H O W T O

Help your child make the most of school

HOW TO

Help your child make the most of school

TERRI FIELDS

FISHER
BOOKS

Publishers: Bill Fisher
             Helen Fisher
             Howard Fisher
             Tom Monroe, P.E.
Cover Designed by Josh Young
Designed by Robert Bull Design

Published by Fisher Books
P.O. Box 38040
Tucson, AZ 85740-8040
602/292-9080

*This is an authorized reprint of a
hardcover edition published by Vil-
lard Books, a division of Random
House, Inc.*

**Library of Congress Cataloging-
in-Publication Data**

Fields, Terri, 1948-
  Help your child make the most
of school.

  Includes index.
  1. Home and school—United
States. 2. Education—United
States—Parent participation. 3.
Academic achievement. I. Title.
[LC225.3.F54 1987b] 370.19'3 88-
33575
ISBN 1-55561-022-6

Printed in U.S.A.
Printing 10 9 8 7 6 5 4 3 2

Grateful acknowledgment is made to the following for permission to
reprint previously published material:

Harper & Row, Publishers, Inc.: Adapted selection in "Steps in the SQ3R
Method" from *Effective Study,* Fourth Edition, by Francis P. Robinson.
Copying 1941, 1946 by Harper & Row, Publishers, Inc. Copying 1961,
1970 by Francis P. Robinson. Reprinted by permission of Harper & Row,
Publishers, Inc.

The National Committee for Citizens in Education: Excerpts from the
"Parents Rights Card," and brief summaries of four abstracts from
Parent Participation-Student Achievement: The Evidence Grows, edited
by Anne Henderson (1981). Reprinted with permission of the publisher.

The Riverside Publishing Company: Achievement items based on those
in the Iowa Tests of Basic Skills provided by courtesy of The Riverside
Publishing Company as examples of items used in the Fourth Edition of
the Stanford-Binet Intelligence Scale.

Notice: The information in this book is true and complete to the best of
our knowledge. It is offered with no guarantees on the part of the author
or Fisher Books. The author and publisher disclaim all liability in connection with use of this book.

To my mother, Barbara Bernstein
my husband, Richard
my two children, Lori and Jeffrey

who've made my life so worthwhile

and

To all my students
whose creativity and enthusiasm

have made teaching such a wonderful experience

ABOUT THE AUTHOR

A high school teacher for the past sixteen years, Terri Fields has won numerous teaching awards. They include receiving a Golden Bell for outstanding creativity in motivating students to academic excellence, as well as being named Arizona's Teacher of the Year and Ambassador for Excellence in Education. She has a master of arts degree in secondary education and an honorary doctorate of humane letters.

Terri Fields is also a writer who is a frequent contributor to many national magazines and has received a first-place award from the National Federation of Press Women for educational writing.

Terri, her husband, Rick, and children, Lori, twelve, and Jeffrey, nine, live in Phoenix, Arizona.

ACKNOWLEDGMENTS

There are hundreds of parents, teachers, and students to whom I owe a great debt of gratitude for sharing their candid thoughts and feelings about aspects of today's public schools. There's no way I could begin to name them all, but I'd like to give particular appreciation to Pat Andazola, Marc Becker, Jack Barry, Myrna Dunn, Bill Hanlon, Sue Sargusa, Elaine Hostetler, Alan Osbon, Larry Major, Rich Carlberg, Chris Locke, Angela Stannard, Dr. Carol Grosse, Dr. Joel Davidson, the Glendale Union High School District, and the *Captiva crew* of 1986.

A very special thank you to Barbara Herold.

CONTENTS

A NOTE TO THE READER

I have referred to teachers throughout the book as "she" and students as "he." This has not been done to be sexist. It merely helped in terms of clarity. I certainly recognize that many students are female and many fine teachers are male.

INTRODUCTION

I've written *Help Your Child Make the Most of School* for two reasons. First, I've been a teacher all my adult life, and I love my chosen profession. Though I try to make school an interesting journey through learning, I know I can't do it alone. I can see from the faces and the hearts of the thousands of kids I've taught that you, their parents, can be my greatest ally. By working together, we can accomplish so much more for your child.

I've also written this book because of the love I have for my own two children. Not until I had them could I have known how deeply a parent cares and how very much he wants his children to be happy.

I don't believe that any parent wants his child to fail in school, but I know that it's almost impossible to give your child the right kinds of tips and suggestions for success if you don't fully understand the educational system yourself. This book will show you the ways you can make your child's school experiences more productive and successful. Among many other things, it will give you advice on how to improve your child's study skills and test scores; it will help make homework meaningful and achievable; and it will show you how to get involved in your school to create beneficial change for your child.

Quite simply, *Help Your Child Make the Most of School* is meant to stack the deck in favor of every parent who reads it. If you know all about the ways the system works, if you understand all the little things that add up to better grades, you can give your child the edge he so richly deserves.

I believe in America's public school system. I believe in your children as our future, and I believe in you as a caring parent. So welcome to the inside of the educational world. Read carefully, and know that the understanding you've gained can reflect itself in your child's triumphs in school.

HELP YOUR CHILD MAKE THE MOST OF SCHOOL

ONE

THE PARENT-TEACHER CONFERENCE: *How to Make It Productive Instead of Painful*

Parent-teacher conferences are supposed to be a time when people vitally interested in a child's welfare sit down together to talk about how to best maximize that child's learning, but is that how you really feel about the piece of paper that beckons you to school to discuss your child? If the answer is no, you're probably not alone in your feelings. In fact, you may be surprised to know that the very teacher who sent the note may not be looking forward to the meeting either.

Why not? Let's eavesdrop on a faculty meeting at one elementary school. The principal hands out the conference forms and announces, "For those of you who are new on our faculty, I want to stress our dedication to these twice-a-year, scheduled parent-teacher conferences. Please encourage your students to have their parents attend. Last year, we had an excellent parent turnout, and I'm counting on this year's faculty to do even better."

3

Sandy, a long-time third-grade teacher, looks over her forms and sighs. "I don't know why they call them conferences," she says. "From my experience, they ought to call them parent-teacher confrontations."

Many parents would agree with that assessment. In fact, that's not their only complaint. Ask Mrs. Johnson, Mr. and Mrs. Turbesh, or Mrs. Alexander about scheduled, routine parent-teacher conferences. All three of them will tell you that such conferences are a total waste of time, and they base their opinions on more than just idle speculation. Each has recently finished with such a conference and left it wondering why he'd bothered to come at all.

MAKING ORDINARY CONFERENCES EXTRAORDINARY

Most elementary schools schedule parent-teacher conferences at the end of at least one grading period during the year. In theory such conferences are a great idea, but in practice, they leave many teachers and parents feeling quite frustrated. Does that mean that such routine conferences should be totally abandoned?

Not at all. As a parent, you owe it to yourself and your child to find out how he's progressing in school. The question then becomes how can you make infrequent and brief parent-teacher conferences productive?

Mrs. Johnson, Mr. and Mrs. Turbesh, and Mrs. Alexander aren't sure such a thing is possible. They know they did their best, but perhaps there is much to be learned from listening in on each of their conferences to find out just what went wrong and why.

Mrs. Johnson arrived for her son Eric's first-grade conference feeling nervous and ill at ease at the thought of having to talk with a teacher. In an effort to avoid silence and establish rapport with the teacher, Mrs. Johnson began making small talk. "The weather's been so bad the last couple of weeks. Do the children miss going outside?"

"Well, somewhat," replied Eric's teacher, and with that she began a careful explanation of the indoor physical education and rainy day free-time programs the school had established. Upon finishing, she glanced at her watch. "Mrs. Johnson, I'm afraid we've about run out of time. Here is Eric's report card. He's a darling little boy. As you can see from his reading grade, you may want to work with him a little more at home." With that she stood, indicating the end of the conference.

Mrs. Johnson noticed that other people were waiting for the teacher. Smiling, she took the report card, thanked the teacher, and left. By the time she got to the car, she was feeling quite frustrated. "I don't care anything about the PE program," she thought, "and I don't know what's wrong with Eric's reading or what I'm supposed to do about it. What's the matter with that teacher that she is putting so much emphasis on PE when my Eric needs to learn to read?"

Ironically, the teacher had no idea Mrs. Johnson was frustrated. In fact, the teacher felt good about the conference, patting herself on the back for being flexible enough to put aside her prepared comments and focus in on Mrs. Johnson's anxieties about physical education. She wished Mrs. Johnson had been more concerned about reading, but the principal had encouraged teachers to be responsive to parent questions and at least now Mrs. Johnson wouldn't worry that the weather was stopping Eric from increased motor-development skills.

How to keep such mistakes from happening to you? First, realize that the idea of mandated, scheduled conferences is to get you to the school, to have you meet the teacher, see the classroom, and get a brief idea of what your child's report card means. Since teachers are given only one to two days for the entire class's conferences, these meetings must be necessarily short. Therefore, the first tip toward creating a successful parent-teacher conference is making sure you arrive a few minutes early; coming five minutes late to a fifteen-minute conference means you've missed a third of it. Frequently, the exact time length will be stated on the note announcing the conference. If it isn't, call the school and ask so that you'll know going in how much time you'll have with the teacher.

Realize that because the conference is not going to be very lengthy, you don't have time for small talk. Before you go in to the conference sit down and decide what your concerns and questions are. Prioritize them, and get right to the first one. In Mrs. Johnson's case, she had no real concerns going into the conference, so she should have let the teacher begin immediately. Then as soon as the teacher had brought up the problem with reading, Mrs. Johnson could have focused on asking what the teacher could suggest at home and at school to help Eric improve.

If your conference has ended, but you still have more questions, give the teacher a few days to finish the rest of the scheduled conferences and then call her with a request for an appointment. At the second conference you won't have such limited time constraints, and you can discuss your child in a more thorough manner. However, it is still important to plan exactly what questions you need answered, and come prepared. As one second-grade teacher implored, "Please, tell parents to stick to things relating to school. If there has been a divorce or a death or something happening at home that would suddenly affect a child's schoolwork, I want to know about it, but last week, for example, I had stacks of papers sitting on my desk just waiting to be graded, and a mother came in and spent a half hour telling me how her two kids were driving her crazy because they kept fighting at home, and did I have any suggestions to stop their behavior. I tried to be polite, but I resented what she was doing."

Mr. and Mrs. Turbesh went to their parent-teacher conference about Annie determined to make it productive. Quite worried about their six-grade daughter's math performance, the couple wanted it to be the focus of the conference. Fortunately, Annie's teacher began by showing the couple their child's report card and explaining, "As you can see, this math grade reflects the fact that Annie's having some difficulty with the subject."

"Yes, but I can't understand why!" Mr. Turbesh affirmed. "Annie's a bright girl." Before the teacher could respond, Mrs. Turbesh quickly added that she'd always had math phobias herself as a child and that her husband simply didn't understand how intimidating math could be or how upsetting it was to Annie to know her father was angry with her.

Annie's teacher suggested that Annie might be able to learn more and keep up better in a little slower math group, but Mr. Turbesh objected immediately. "If you could just stress that she's got to pay more attention and stop daydreaming . . ."

"Oh, I don't know," interrupted Mrs. Turbesh, "if she does daydream, I think it's because she gets so confused."

Mr. and Mrs. Turbesh continued their discussion, each becoming more firm in his position. The teacher glanced at her watch. She had to go on to the next conference. She could only end by saying that she was pleased they all agreed that something needed to be done about Annie's math situation. "I'd be happy to put Annie in a slower moving group. Why don't you let me know if that's the direction you want to go."

The couple left, and Mr. Turbesh turned to his wife. "See, I told you that teacher wasn't going to be much help. She didn't have anything to contribute. We had to do all the talking, and I still don't know what we're going to do about Annie's math problem."

Sound farfetched? Then listen to the words of this veteran fourth-grade teacher. Having taught for the past twenty years, she's seen many changes, including the appearance of more fathers at parent-teacher conferences. She says, "While I'm delighted to see fathers taking more of an interest in their children's education, often a couple arrives and spends the whole conference talking to each other. I almost feel rude to interrupt. Furthermore, the dynamics are such that I usually feel as if I'm being put in the position of siding with one parent or the other. I hate it. I wish they'd talk things over at home before they arrive. It may sound ridiculous, but sometimes I have the feeling that with busy, two-parent working families, they're using the conference to sit down and communicate with each other."

Of course, parents aren't the only ones responsible for a conference that fails. Though parents often feel intimidated by returning to the classrooms and sitting on chairs designed for people half their size, they don't realize that many teachers are equally intimidated by these conferences. "I love kids. I do not love parents," was the comment overheard in one faculty workroom. It was quickly agreed to by the other teachers.

The teacher continued, "In college, I learned to teach math and reading; how to handle discipline and raise a child's self-esteem. I never learned anything about dealing with parents, and I never really know what to say to them."

Perhaps that's why Mrs. Alexander had a problem. Arriving at her daughter Melanie's conference, she took out a notebook. "I hope you don't mind," she said, "but if I take notes, it will help me keep track of what you've said."

Twenty minutes later, Mrs. Alexander sat in her car examining her notes carefully. They made no sense. They mentioned the CAT, the WISC, a SCIIS, and something about a minimal dysfunction. Mrs. Alexander had never really considered herself stupid, but she couldn't understand any of the information. It seemed to be written in a language other than English.

Unfortunately, she was the victim of what we who are long-time teachers call "educationalese" or "alphabet speak." It happens for two reasons. Sometimes, beginning teachers who are unsure of themselves use big terms to hide behind. They think it makes them sound more professional and makes them less likely to be challenged or questioned by parents.

However, it's not only beginning teachers who get caught up in educationalese. Veteran teachers can become so familiar with these terms that they no longer seem strange or foreign, and they simply forget that the average person has little reason to come in contact with such terminology or acronyms. Such teachers don't mean to be confusing to the parent; in fact they don't realize that they aren't being perfectly clear.

Whatever the reason, it's important that you as the parent make sure that you break through all this unnecessary jargon. The best way to do this is simply to ask the teacher what she means, and not to give up if you don't understand the explanation. For example, if she's talking about your child's science grade and keeps referring to SCIIS, ask her what the SCIIS is. If she replies only by telling you what the initials stand for, and that isn't enough explanation, continue to ask questions. If you're polite, but persistent, you'll break through the educationalese, and both you and your child will be better off because of it.

PRECONFERENCE PLANNING

The parent-teacher conference is one way for you to forge a link to your child's school, and it can be quite successful if you understand how to prepare and how to handle it. Mark this page, and before you go to your conference, review these items.

- Look over your child's completed assignments. See what type of work he has been doing in school. Write down any questions you have. For example, are his reading papers very erratic with all questions answered correctly one day and many missed the next day? Does his work look sloppy to you? How often does he bring home completed work? If it seems as if not much is filtering home, make a note to ask the teacher what she is sending home. Perhaps much of it is disappearing along the way.

- Glance through your child's textbooks. Social studies, for example, is a very broad area. His textbooks can give you a much better idea of what he's actually studying, and to what his grades are relating. For example, is his book looking primarily at world geography or American history? Having perused his books, you'll be in tune with what is being taught, and you'll be able to ask the teacher intelligent questions about it.

- Ask your child if there's anything he'd like you to tell his teacher. Invite him to share in the process of evaluating his school experience. Your child's comments and questions will help you decide what you want to talk about with the teacher as well as make the child feel a part of the conference process.

- Look over past report cards to refresh your memory about your child's possible strengths and weaknesses. Look not only at academic grades but at behavior and effort as well. Reread any comments the teachers have written. Remember though, different teachers grade entirely differently, and just because he got A's in language last year and is getting C's this year does not mean he's falling behind. It could just be a difference in his teachers' standards. However, the situation is worth checking out, and during the conference you might want to ask the teacher some specific questions about what's being covered in language this year.

- Most schools have a parent/student handbook which unfortunately often remains unread by parents. Before you go to your conference, skim the handbook. It may answer many of your questions about the routines and expectations of the school and leave you more conference time to discuss specific things about your child. Glancing through the handbook may also create new questions you want answered.

- Make a list of all the questions you have for the teacher, and then pick out the few that you feel are most important. Some questions you might want to consider:

  a) How much time a night do you feel your students should spend on homework? Is my child getting his assignments completed on time?

  b) Does my child seem to get along with the other kids in the class?

  c) Does my child need any extra help? If so, in what areas, and are there support people at this school who can provide that help?

  d) Do you feel that my child is doing satisfactorily in accomplishing the basic skills?

  e) Have you noticed any major changes in my child's academic ability or social or physical behavior?

  f) Is there anything I as a parent can do at home to help make my child more successful in school?

- If you think you may get sidetracked or tongue-tied, write down the questions you most want answered and take them into the conference with you. Don't be embarrassed to do this. It is our responsibility as teachers to answer the questions you have, and you actually make our job easier when you verbalize specific concerns.

- As the teacher is explaining things to you, ask questions if you don't understand. You have the right to know what she is saying. For example, if she mentions that your son always seems to finish his reading faster than anyone in the class, and you're not sure whether she's telling you that he's very bright or that he's not really reading the material, you need to ask her a question of clarification. When she answers, continue to ask questions until you feel you've got an accurate picture.

- Even if you think you are understanding the teacher's comments, it doesn't hurt to paraphrase from time to time to make certain that you are hearing what she's saying in the way she is intending it.

- If the conference ends, and you still have questions, don't try to squeeze in just one more thing. Instead, make an appointment for another day when the teacher can devote more time to you. Remember that the conferences are usually scheduled fairly tightly, and if you stick around after yours is supposed to end, you may make the teacher run behind for the rest of the evening. Because she knows this is happening, she cannot give you the full attention your questions deserve.

- Immediately after the conference, sit down and make notes for yourself as to what you and the teacher actually said. Without notes, you may later forget or misinterpret some important point.

- When you get home, give your child some feedback. Try to find at least one positive thing that the teacher said about him. If the teacher said that your child is polite and well mannered, he'd probably enjoy hearing that as much as you did. In concentrating on what needs to be improved, parents often forget to also reveal the compliments their children have received. Yet, ironically, one good way to encourage positive behavior is to recognize it and praise it. You and the teacher are some of the most important authority figures in your child's life; it will make him feel great to know that you're both proud of something about him.

- After you return from a conference, be sure to tell your child that you enjoyed talking with his teacher. If your child thinks that you found the experience a waste of time, his attitude toward his teacher is likely to reveal it. That doesn't mean you should be phony and gush over a teacher you didn't particularly care for, but since your child will be in her class every day for the rest of the year, it might be helpful to the child if you could find one positive thing to say about his teacher.

IT'S OPEN HOUSE!

Primarily, only elementary schools have the regularly scheduled conferences that have been discussed above. Unfortunately, most junior and senior high schools forego them, not because they don't believe that such a program would be valuable, but because sheer numbers preclude their being realistically possible. Whereas an elementary school teacher may have the same thirty children all day, a high school teacher may have as many as 170 kids each day. Not only would it be staggering for her to try to conference 170 parents, but parents would have quite a task ahead of them as well. Most high school students have six classes a day. That would mean that even if the parent spent only fifteen minutes with each teacher, he'd spend over two hours at school having conferences.

Perhaps some parents see the lack of planned conferences as a hint that they should withdraw from their children's school. Whether for this reason or because of increased school size or the fact that the children are older and seem to want more independence, the drop in parental participation is something almost every junior high and high school notices. Even parents who have actively been involved in the PTA in their child's elementary school often stay away from the high school, but it's definitely a mistake. Though they may be reluctant to show it, kids need their parents more than ever through the teenage years, and one good way to stay in contact with the school is to make certain you attend the school's open house or back-to-school night. Unfortunately, most high schools get far less response to this evening than they'd like. A first-grade room is always packed on such a night. A high school class may have only a few parents. Yet national research shows that kids do better when their parents are involved in school. My own sixteen years in the classroom substantiate this. The parents of my A students are almost always there; the parents of my indifferent students never seem to make it to open house.

While an open house is certainly not as personal as a conference, it can give you a feel for the school. In most cases, an open house or back-to-school night is held very early in the school year and gives you the opportunity to follow your child's schedule and spend about five to ten minutes in each of his classes. The teacher gives an overview of what she is going to be doing for the year. Many parents fail to attend open house because they feel that it is not personalized enough to make their attendance worthwhile. It is easy to see why parents conditioned by years of individual elementary school conferences would feel this way, but there is much to be gained from attending a school's open house. You can see each teacher, hear the way she speaks, and find out what kinds of requirements, both in terms of academic effort and citizenship, that she expects from the students in her class as well as the material that she intends to cover in her course. By knowing a little about the teacher's personality and rules, you may be able to help your child throughout the year. For example, when Molly, an eighth grader, began complaining that she was always getting in trouble in her junior high history class and she couldn't figure out why Mr. Kenton picked on her, her mother thought back to the open house. "Don't you have history class right after science?" she asked.

"Yeah," said Molly, "but I love science, and I never get in trouble in there."

Even during the ten-minute class periods of open house, Molly's mother had been struck by the difference in the two men's classrooms and teaching styles, and it was clearly apparent to her what was causing Molly's problem. Through her mother's gentle questioning, Molly was soon able to realize that while her science teacher used humor to make his points and liked an open, spirited class in which anyone could call out, her history teacher was quite regimented and viewed talking out as disrespect. "I guess," said Molly, "I'm still bringing the sort of silly me from science into history." With that realization in mind, Molly and her history teacher began getting along much better.

Explained her mother, "I'd never have known that was the issue if I'd just seen an unsatisfactory in behavior in history on her report card. In fact, I wouldn't have known why Molly was having trouble in history even if I'd scheduled a conference with the history teacher. It was only readily apparent to me because I'd gone through Molly's schedule on back-to-school night."

Another advantage of attending such an evening is that because the event is held so early in the school year, parents can be alerted to possible problems before they've ever surfaced in another way. For example, if each teacher says he's assigning about fifteen to thirty minutes of homework a night and your child has been maintaining he has none, you can investigate and perhaps alter some poor study habits long before the results show up as negative report card grades. In Cindy's case, the computer had scheduled her into remedial English instead of average English. Her mother hadn't known about the error; the teacher hadn't caught it; and because there was a cute boy in the class, Cindy hadn't said anything either. Cindy's high school had its open house the third week of school, and fortunately, her mother attended and was able to get Cindy in the class she belonged before her daughter had spent too much time in a class that was far too easy for her.

Finally, the last good reason for attending an open house is that it gives you more of a chance to open communication with the teacher. That works two ways. The teacher who sees you sitting in the classroom may well be tempted to pass along specific information about your child that isn't really important enough to warrant a phone call—yet. On the other hand, being right there may make you more likely to set up a conference with a teacher you've been meaning to call.

THE PARENT-REQUESTED CONFERENCE

"Why," said one incredulous woman, "would parents want to call kids' teachers if the kids haven't gotten in any trouble?" The answer is simple. As a parent you cannot simply assume that if your child is having any difficulties, the teacher will let you know. Even the most caring teacher still has a multitude of kids to consider each day; she cannot catch everything. If you've got questions or concerns that need answers, please contact her.

There are, however, some steps that will either sabotage such a conference or send it on its way to success. Consider into which category Nina's mother fits.

Nine-year-old Nina arrived home one day, went to her room, lay down on her bed, and began to sob. After much coaxing she tearfully told her mother, "Mrs. Allen chose people for the play today, and me and Jennifer tried for the lead, and Mrs. Allen said she couldn't decide, and she let the class decide, and they picked Jennifer. All the other parts got taken, and now I don't get to be in the play at all. I didn't get to be in one play all year."

Nina's mother attempted to soothe Nina, but she found herself getting more and more agitated. The next morning she packed Nina off to school, and stormed into the principal's office. No one was going to push her child around like this. The principal was on his way to another conference but agreed to see Nina's mother the following afternoon. Leaving the school, Nina's mother felt angry and frustrated with her inability to immediately do something about her daughter's hurt.

All day Nina's mother worried; how could she tell her daughter she had no solution yet? However, much to her surprise, that afternoon Nina came home smiling. She and four other kids in the class had been chosen to put on a puppet show, and the art teacher was going to help them make puppets. Nina's mother was confused. "But I thought you said everyone else was in the play? Aren't you still upset about not getting the lead?"

Nina shrugged. "Why would I want to be in that dumb play, when I can do a puppet show for the whole fifth grade?" Sheepishly, her mother canceled the appointment with the principal.

Nina's mother is certainly not to blame for her feelings. No parent wants to see his child upset or unhappy, but unless the problem is critical, it's better to wait a few days before scheduling a conference about it. Kids do tend to see things in terms of immediate crisis, and what they stew about one day may be gone and forgotten the next. You can't fight their every battle; it's not even healthy to try. Save your steam for the times that it really matters.

On the other hand, if a problem persists for more than a few days, you shouldn't feel intimidated or reluctant to take a teacher's time for a conference. Many difficulties could be kept from escalating if they were handled before they reached such large proportions. When Jonathan began complaining that he was getting headaches in music, his mother didn't pay much attention; however, when ten days had passed, and he was still complaining, his mother decided that whether they be from some physical or emotional reason, it was time to do something about them. Making an appointment with the music teacher, she discovered that Jonathan's headaches had started just about the time he'd been moved to a different seat in music. Working with the teacher and confronting Jonathan, his mother discovered that he was being teased and intimidated by the boy who'd been moved behind him. Another seating change and Jonathan's headaches miraculously disappeared.

Knowing when to request a conference is the first step in making it successful. Knowing what to say is step number two. Keep teamwork in mind, and don't get caught using any of the techniques that are bound to antagonize the teacher. Begin by calling the school and asking the teacher to return your phone call. Don't call the teacher at home, and don't just show up at the school. You may think it would be more informal if you just stopped in, but teachers don't see it quite that way. True, the teacher may be sitting at her desk in an empty classroom twenty minutes before school starts, but chances are she's there because she's allotted this time for last minute preparations of some aspect of the day's activities. Your arrival will throw all that off, and the teacher is likely to be less than enthusiastic about talking with you. Not only will her mind be elsewhere, but her time will be so limited that she won't be able to give you the attention you deserve.

In your initial phone call, remember to leave your work and home phone numbers, your last name if it differs from your child's, and some idea of the reason that you want to talk to the teacher. You don't have to give every detail, but it will save you time and make the teacher's return call more productive if she knows what you're concerned about.

By calling, leaving this information, and waiting for a return call, you can be assured that the teacher can select a time to talk with you when she can focus her attention specifically on you and your child. Furthermore, she can check through her gradebook and other sources to make certain that she has ready information about your child at her fingertips.

Not too long ago, I was at a party with a woman who, when she heard that I was Arizona's Teacher of the Year, began telling me of how she'd gotten the upper hand with her child's teacher. "I had some questions about my son's schoolwork, so I called his teacher for an appointment." Her voice took on a gleeful tone. "The secretary asked me what it was in reference to, but I wouldn't tell her anything. In fact, since I've remarried recently, the teacher probably didn't even know who I was. I'm sure I caught her totally off guard, which is just what I wanted to do! That way she couldn't just plan some whole story about my son."

I shook my head sadly. This woman had perceived the teacher as the enemy instead of seeing her as part of a team effort to educate her child. I could only tell the woman that if I needed to request a conference for one of my own children, I'd want to give the teacher as much information as possible beforehand. I'd want her to pull papers, review grades, and focus in on my child.

If for some reason you don't want your child to know that you've called for a conference, be sure to mention it when you call. Otherwise, the teacher may tell the child that you've contacted her and ask him about it. I'd advise, however, that unless there is some specific reason not to, you really should involve your child both in knowing about the conference, and perhaps in attending it. He should not see that his education is others' responsibility; he should learn at an early age to be an accountable part of his own learning.

Once you have called the teacher, give her several days to return your call; however, if you haven't heard from her in a reasonable period of time, call back. Occasionally, a message is lost, given to the wrong teacher, or even forgotten. Also, for some teachers it is as nervewracking to get a message that a parent called as it is for a parent to get a message that the teacher called, and so they put off making a return call. Don't be embarrassed to follow through with a second call.

After telephone contact has been made with the teacher, you may decide that it would be better to set up a face-to-face conference, and you should request it at that time. It's also appropriate to decide whether you should have your child or any of the school resource people attend the scheduled meeting. Your time is valuable, and having all the necessary people at a conference can save you frustration and accomplish much more in a limited amount of time.

Many problems arise in parent-requested conferences because the parent doesn't voice his concerns to the teacher before pursuing other avenues. In spite of how aggravated you may be or how unfair you feel the teacher is, don't go straight to the principal. You may think this action will expedite the problem, but usually it just aggravates it. No one appreciates having to defend himself in front of his boss without first getting the chance to straighten things out himself. The teacher who might have been perfectly willing to admit that she made a mistake had you gone directly to her now feels compelled to try to explain her actions in front of her boss. Instead of working for what's best for your child, the teacher is defending herself and her work.

The principal, too, is caught in a quandary. He feels that he must hear all the facts from all sides, and that to an extent, he must support his faculty as well as keeping his community happy. Realize that if things don't go well with the teacher, you can always go higher in your complaints, not only to the principal but onward to the school district and board of education. However, before doing this, at least satisfy yourself that you tried for a quicker, cleaner solution by first dealing with the teacher.

What sorts of problems might make you seek a conference with a teacher? Consider:

• Your child suddenly starts complaining that no one in his class likes him, and he seems never to have any friends over any more. Perhaps he's begun to manifest behavior that while it doesn't affect his academic performance needs to be dealt with in terms of his social growth.

• A serious personal or family problem has arisen that may affect your child's behavior in school. Teachers can often be supportive of a student who is trying to deal with a parent's death or divorce. I particularly remember one of my sophomore girls. Bubbly and gregarious, she became totally withdrawn after her father's unexpected death. After talking with her mother, I called the girl in. Her father had been a fine photographer, and I asked if I could use some of his slides for a creative-writing unit. She shyly brought them in, and my students wrote beautiful pieces describing his pictures. When the unit was finished, she came in to talk to me about all that her father had taught her about photography, and she made me copies of the slides to keep in case I wanted to use them in future years. "It makes me feel better to know that kids will keep writing such special things based on Dad's pictures." After that she began to join in more class activities again. I was glad that I could have helped her, but I could never have done so without the teamwork of her concerned mother.

- Your child's academic work suddenly worsens. Even if he has some explanation for this, you may want to check into it, especially if you have a feeling that you're not getting the whole story from him or he seems to be completing all the homework successfully.

- Your child will have to be out of school for several days or longer. Find out what you can do in terms of getting his homework, and helping him keep up. Again and again, I have seen the direct value of this. Recently, two boys in my class were out of school for a week with a bad flu bug. The one whose mother had arranged for his assignments to be sent home returned to school not only feeling physically healthy, but able to keep up and continue with the class. The other boy waited until he returned to get all his makeup work and went home from school that day feeling overwhelmed and defeated.

- You feel that you strongly disagree with something that the teacher said in class or with a particular facet of the curriculum. While you certainly don't want to descend on the school every time you have a difference of opinion with a teacher's comment, you shouldn't let things which really offend your basic beliefs go unchallenged. Make an appointment with the teacher; arrive without anger, and see if you can find out what was really said or done, and if at that point, you still disagree with it, explain your position. Such conferences should be handled in a calm, reasonable, intellectual atmosphere, but instead, they are frequently emotionally charged. Try to keep the emotionalism out of the conference, and you'll accomplish more. If you're still unhappy when the conference ends, go home and evaluate whether you wish to pursue the matter further, and if so, what would be the most logical way to proceed.

THE TEACHER-REQUESTED CONFERENCE

To most parents there are few things more rattling than picking up the phone to unexpectedly hear, "This is your child's teacher, and I believe that we need to discuss a problem he is having."

"My heart dropped down to my feet," shuddered Mary, the mother of eleven-year-old Jordan, in recalling such a phone call from her son's teacher. "I was so stunned by her comments that Jordan was bullying other children. I know he can be rather rambunctious, but he's really a good kid. I confess that part of me didn't even want to hear what his teacher was saying. Besides, she caught me just as I was making dinner, and the television was blaring from the other room. The commotion in the house and my surprise at the teacher's call made it hard to concentrate on her exact words. Flustered, I just said that Jordan had never had any trouble in school before, and maybe discipline needed to be tighter in her class. The teacher, an icy-cold tone in her voice, informed me that part of her discipline plan was to have Jordan stay after school every day the following week, and she just wanted me to know about it."

Obviously, this was not a good conference. The teacher was angry; the parent was distraught. What could have made it better?

First of all, when you hear the teacher on the other end of the phone, promise yourself that you will not react; instead, you will just listen to what she has to say. If the teacher has caught you at a hectic time, or if you just feel stunned or confused by what she is saying, tell her you appreciate her calling and that you are concerned and would like to set up a time when you could meet to discuss the situation further. In that way, you'll have a chance to think things over. You haven't suddenly been put on the spot to arrive at a solution; instead, you'll have time to act based on what's best for your child. You can sit down and think over what the teacher has told you, talk to your child, and view some of his work before you meet with the teacher.

Though it doesn't necessarily make it any easier for a parent to get bad news about his child, it should be remembered that it is really hard for most teachers to have to be the bearers of that news. As one seventh-grade social studies teacher said only half jokingly, "In ancient times, they used to kill the bearer of bad tidings. Sometimes, I think parents would still like to subscribe to that theory."

It is easy to react negatively. In some ways, parents tend to feel as if they themselves have been attacked when their child has gotten in trouble. Try to remember that no teacher expects you to have the answers to all the questions, and that just because your child has gotten in trouble doesn't mean you aren't a good or loving parent.

One teacher said she made a list of the responses she hated the most. "Every time I call a parent to say his child is having trouble and he responds with one of these, I can tell we're going nowhere."

Here are some of teachers' least favorite parental responses to hearing that there might be problems with their children. Though it's certainly understandable what motivates parents to say these things, it's also important to see how they contribute to a catastrophic parent-teacher conference.

- "Frankly, I'm quite surprised. My daughter has always really enjoyed school before she got to your class." (Even if that's true, it only serves to put the teacher on the defensive. Remember that your goal is to get the teacher to work with you to guarantee your child the best possible education.)

- "Are you sure you're describing my son? We simply don't see that kind of behavior at home." (Children are sometimes very different in different environments. The teacher is not talking about dealing with the behavior at home; she wants your help in dealing with the behavior at school.)

- "He must be acting out because he's angry that I'm working, but I have to work." (The implication here is that the parent can't do anything about the source of the problem; therefore, the teacher will just have to deal with the behavior. While there may be some underlying family causes for negative behavior in a child that need to be discussed, this kind of statement is not the best way to begin the conference.)

- "I was the same way when I was a kid. I gave the teachers hell, but eventually, I straightened out." (Great. So the kid's a chip off the old block. What the teacher would like to say is that she's tired of your child's giving her hell, and why don't you keep him until he gets straightened out. It's clear from your tone she'll get no real support from you in handling him.)

- "I agree with everything you've said about my child. He's a real handful around here too. He never listens to me at all." (The teacher is one main authority figure in your child's life. You are the other. You've just told her that your child has already figured out that he can manipulate you to the point that he needs to pay no attention to you at all. In what kind of position does that leave her?)

If those are the things you *shouldn't* say, what should you say to make a teacher-initiated conference successful? Assuming you've taken the time to think about what the teacher has said, and you've organized your own thoughts before the meeting, walk in with the promise that you plan to get the facts. Later, you may agree or disagree, but first you have to get the information so that you can accurately assess the situation. For example, Janine's teacher says, "I've called you because I'm concerned that Janine simply isn't applying herself in math."

You say, "I appreciate your concern. Could you be more specific?"

The teacher will respond, but if you're still not certain what is being said, paraphrase the teacher's words. If she's said that Janine is too relaxed during math, you might say, "Is what you are saying that Janine isn't paying attention during math instruction?"

Keep working at it until you know just what the teacher perceives as the exact problem. If this seems rather time-consuming and laborious, remember that many teachers are gun shy. They couch bad news in euphemistic terms because they're tired of being attacked and hope to blunt parents' negative reactions. Obviously, these veiled comments often result in confused communication.

Once you do understand the problem, it is important that you and the teacher and perhaps even your child work together on a solution. Just because she's the teacher doesn't mean she has all the answers. Be fair, but don't be afraid to add your own ideas.

Finally, don't feel that you must simply "give in" to the teacher. If after all the information has been presented, you still disagree with her assessment, try to state why objectively. For example, I once recommended a student drop out of the accelerated English program. Making the call to her parents was not easy. Her mother's first reaction was that she'd hoped this phone call would never come; however, she appreciated my concern and wanted to talk to me.

We set up an appointment. I showed the mother her daughter's papers and her grades and discussed why I felt she should be out of the program. "I really feel that it's putting undue stress on her to work so hard and only get C's and D's," I concluded. "School should be a rewarding experience, and I don't think she's getting enough reward for the amount of work she's putting in."

The mother listened carefully. She acknowledged the points I had made. Then she said that she'd spoken at length with her daughter; they'd reviewed many of the papers together, and she began to factually and yet pleasantly present her position. By the time she was finished, I agreed, based on some of her reflections about her daughter, that we should leave the child in the accelerated program for the time being.

This mother continued to monitor her daughter's progress. She asked if I'd mind filling out a one- or two-sentence evaluation on her child's work each Friday. I was happy to do so, for the last rule of a good parent-teacher conference concerns follow-up. Big problems are rarely resolved all at once, and simply saying, "Please call me if anything else is wrong," just isn't sufficient. With 150 other students in class each day, the teacher may not get back to you about your child unless there is another pressing problem. Working out some quick but definite evaluation form makes far more sense. You can help your child be involved in this by giving him the responsibility of giving the teacher the evaluation note each week.

When the conference ends, be sure to express your appreciation to the teacher for taking the time and interest to meet with you. Teachers are human too, and they appreciate positive feedback.

Parent-teacher conferences don't have to be terrible. Whether it is a regularly mandated conference, a parent-initiated one, or a teacher-requested meeting, the purpose should be to achieve effective communication. Following the tips in this chapter should enable you to work as part of a caring team with your child's school. A successful parent-teacher conference allows you and the teacher to better understand your child and to be able to best meet his educational needs.

*T*WO

PARENTS COME BACK! WE NEED YOU: Your Role in Today's Schools

Most parents begin worrying about their child and school long before an official parent-teacher conference. How well I remember that day I sent my daughter to school for the first time. "School is going to be wonderful," I reassured her, crossing my fingers so that my words wouldn't be a lie. "I know you're going to love it." I walked my child into her classroom, hating to let go of her hand even more than she hated to let go of mine. I introduced her to her teacher and then reluctantly realized that it was time for me to leave. Waving bravely and putting a smile on my face, I walked out the door, went home, and paced the floor. Agonizingly, I hoped that the teachers would see how truly wonderful my little girl was. She liked to be read to, but she didn't like to play ball. She liked to skip, but she didn't want to be made to run. Would they discover that? Would these teachers be kind to my baby?

The house seemed woefully silent without my daughter. The morning seemed to take forever to pass, but at least there was some solace. It came from the many phone calls of other preschoolers' nervous mothers.

26

Have you been nodding your head in remembrance of your own child's first day at school? If so, you've probably got lots of company. Most mothers feel that lump in their throats as their children begin school, and it's easy to see why. We love our children; for the first few years of their lives we participate in or make every decision about them, and yet, ironically, as soon as they reach school age we frequently send them off to school feeling as if it is a domain which we cannot or should not enter.

This hit home to me again the other night at a cocktail party. The hostess introduced me to a couple I didn't know, and trying to establish a common ground, she said, "This is Terri Fields. She teaches at Sunnyslope."

"Oh, our son goes there," said his father with obvious pride in the child. "I can't say that I know any of the teachers though, because Jason is a terrific kid. He's never gotten in any trouble at all."

I thought of the parent club, the open houses, and the other opportunities for involvement, and I mentioned them to this man, but he waved me aside. "Oh, my wife and I don't really have time for all that stuff. Besides, what do we know about running a high school?"

WHY GET INVOLVED?

Though a busy schedule and feelings of uncertainty are two major reasons parents don't get involved in their child's school, the rewards are worth the effort. Being a caring parent makes a big difference. Not only can it help provide your child with a better education, but it reinforces the idea that school is an important place as far as the entire family is concerned. Additionally, your involvement can make programs and processes available that improve the quality of education for all the children of the school.

Dr. Carol Grosse, Superintendent of Alhambra Elementary School District in Arizona, explains, "Schools are designed around the concept of democracy. They can only be as successful as parents view education important. Parents definitely can and should take the opportunity to have input in curriculum, text selection, and school system changes. I believe that parents certainly care as much or more than they ever have about education, but they must realize that to ensure the best schooling for their children, that caring has to translate into active involvement."

THE HIDDEN BENEFITS OF PARTICIPATING IN YOUR CHILD'S SCHOOL

There are many ways for you to become involved in your school. For starters, there is still a need for the traditional role of the homeroom mother. Her stated duties may be to call parents of students in the class for certain events, to assist the teacher in planning parties for the children at particular times of the year, and sometimes to assist on field trips. The unstated benefits, however, are the reasons to take on the job. It allows a parent closer contact with the teacher which may make the parent feel much more comfortable about talking with the teacher about his own child. It allows the parent to see how other children in the class act, and it tells the child that the parent is interested in what's going on in his classroom.

All of these benefits and more are available to parents who work as volunteer parent aides in their children's classroom. Sitting in the back of the classroom, these parents may grade papers, help children with makeup work, provide an ear to listen to a slow reader practice, etc. The best part about the work is that seldom do these parents need to depend on twice-a-year conferences to know how their children are interacting socially, emotionally, or intellectually in the classroom. Mom or Dad is there once a week and sees whether his child is the one who never raises his hand, who is consistently getting the highest scores in spelling, etc.

Parents who have expertise in a particular area may choose to invest in the school system by sharing that expertise. A computer programmer who'd been an amateur folk singer during his college days volunteered to come to his children's school and teach the kids folk songs. He gathered the children in a circle on the floor, sat down among them with his guitar, and began to sing. His son's mouth dropped open in awe and admiration, and the child's friends spent the next week telling the boy how lucky he was to have such a neat dad. As nice an ending as the story has, it almost didn't happen because the father felt embarrassed, and debated about even offering his services.

Another example comes in the woman who was a busy architect. When the PTA at her school raised money for playground equipment, she volunteered to design the playground for them. Bringing home the blueprints and plans, she explained to her daughter what she was doing. Aside from the pride the child felt in the completed playground, the message she got was clear. Her mom cared about this school, and therefore, it must be an important place.

You may feel that you don't have that kind of special talent, but whatever your job, chances are you can be a valuable resource person to your child's school. A personnel manager came to a high school English class feeling somewhat uncertain of himself, beginning to wish he hadn't agreed to come. He couldn't understand why kids would want to listen to him talk about his job. However, as the English teacher had requested, he brought a number of applications that he'd recently received to review with the students. Putting the first one on an opaque projector, he explained that he wouldn't hire this person because the application contained three spelling errors and two bad grammatical errors, and if she couldn't even properly complete an application, she surely couldn't represent the company well. There was an audible gasp from some of the raptly attentive students.

The father who'd come was surprised that he'd gotten such an attentive response, but the teacher wasn't. She explained that every sixteen-year-old would love to have his own car, and that in order to get the car, most teens needed jobs. This man was telling them how to get or not get those jobs. Talking about grammar, punctuation, and spelling were things she did every day, but his coming had suddenly made English relevant to the "real world." She could tell the kids that using correct English mattered on applications, but many of the kids shrugged and said that it was a teacher-type thing to say. It was entirely different when a real personnel manager was actually rejecting applications based on those things. The hour or two that a parent volunteered about his job provided motivation for a class for the rest of the year.

Parents can also get involved in citizen-advisory groups on a school or more frequently on a district level. These groups consist of parents who are concerned with some of the overriding issues in education. For example, the school board might turn to the citizen-advisory committee to ask for feedback on a potentially sensitive issue such as whether to offer sex education classes or whether to attempt an override election.

Serving on such a committee gives parents a chance to participate in making large decisions and then help communicate them back to the individual schools. For example, in one district it was the citizen-advisory committee who helped make the choice to convert the schools in the district from kindergarten through eighth grade to kindergarten through sixth plus junior high schools. Once the decision was made, this committee was instrumental in communicating the district's timeline to their child's school and answering questions about how the procedure would work.

In short, we in education want you; we need you. As parents and teachers, we share a common interest. We both care very much about your child, and your involvement is necessary to maximize both your child's attitude toward school, and his actual learning.

PARENTS WHOSE PARTICIPATION
MADE A DIFFERENCE

Perhaps it's not enough to hear from educators that you are needed in your child's school. As busy as today's parent is, perhaps it's not even sufficient to simply give examples of the ways you can be involved in your child's education. So let's look at some parents throughout the country who have made the commitment to be

involved. I've asked them what they're getting out of their participation in the schools, and how their children are benefiting. Their
stories follow and may help you decide if your role in your child's
school could be making a big difference in his life.

———————————————

Suzette Wynn is a Phoenix, Arizona, parent who has a nine-
year-old boy and a thirteen-year-old girl. Having spent so many
hours on PTA projects that she no longer can keep count, she's been
the PTA president, Volunteer Parent Instructional Chairman, and
Newsletter Chairman. She says that her work is not all altruistic.
"There are direct benefits to my children. They know by the amount
of time I'm giving to their school how very important their schooling is to me. If I'm going to take it this seriously, they know they
should too. I'm not just telling them school is important, I'm showing them it's so."

She says that by being around all the time, she is able to keep an
eye on her children's education firsthand, and when she feels something is wrong, she can take action before it's too late to do anything
about it. Furthermore, she believes that because of the tremendous
amount of work that she does at the school, when she makes a
request that she thinks will affect her children's well-being, the
school bends over backward to honor it. She knows which teachers
are the most creative, the most stimulating, and the most challenging because she's been there to watch their teaching styles. Though
her stated role at school that day might just be to photocopy for a
teacher, she's also gaining information about the way the school
runs. Finally, she says, "When you're around a lot, and problems
arise, the school looks to you for input into solutions. You're not
the one teaching your child, but you're providing direct suggestions
to help his education."

During the time that she has been involved in her school, she
has seen not only the direct benefits to her own children, but also
the significant improvement for the whole school that involved parents have accomplished. She counts among their accomplishments
getting rid of a principal they considered to be weak and ineffective.

"We marched with petitions, we spoke to district officials, and we worked really hard. The principal is the leader of the school, and we felt there had to be changes made if the school was to be the best it could be."

Currently, parents are working on plans to convince the school to get rid of departmentalization. "We are concerned for two reasons. There seems to be a worsening of discipline, perhaps because the children are spending too little time with any one teacher, and thus, instead of correcting bad behavior, the teacher is tempted to feel that she'll let the next teacher handle the discipline.

"We also support less departmentalization because it seems that our kids are getting the idea that you only spell in spelling; you don't have to worry about correct language usage in science, etc. If one teacher had the children most of the day, he might choose to incorporate a language lesson right into the science lesson. He would know that he just taught them the correct way to spell 'hearty' in spelling, and in creative writing, he would expect the child to spell the word correctly."

In addition to input into the curriculum and the faculty, the PTA at Mrs. Wynn's school raises money to provide things the school needs. They purchased the equipment for a computer laboratory and then made sure it was staffed by providing parent volunteers to give each child the opportunity for computer experience. Mrs. Wynn explains, "It even comes down to something as simple as raising the money for awards, ribbons, and certificates. Maybe that sounds foolish, but we spent almost a thousand dollars on those things last year. The teachers and administration like to be able to give awards to recognize positive accomplishment, but they don't have the funds to buy or the time to make all those awards. I've seen the results of our awards. They may only look like pieces of ribbon to an uninvolved individual, but at our school, receiving an award makes any child feel good about himself; it makes almost any child try harder, and that provides for a more positive school climate for my own children. By being involved in my children's school, I am giving them the best gift that I can give—the chance for a better education."

Barrie Engel is a California attorney and the father of two children, a seven-year-old daughter and a thirteen-year-old son. He is active in his school's PTA, the Kensington Educational Foundation, and the school's Dads' Club. He comments, "I am vitally interested in my children's education, and the only way I see to really know what's going on is to get involved and find out for myself."

He sees primarily two benefits tó his involvement. It's very informational. The Dads' Club meets with the principal once a month to find out what's happening at the school, what the school needs, and what the fathers' concerns are. "School is not something that my children do separate and apart from their mother's and my life. We can discuss it as a family activity because we're all interested; we're all involved."

Equally important, Mr. Engel says, "I believe in public school education, but in California, we've suffered a number of budget cuts. Between Proposition Thirteen and an overall state funding policy, the amount of money available to our school district has dropped tremendously. Partially to combat this, parents staff the school library, plan library programs for each class, and make certain that children feel comfortable with and excited about books.

"I've spent a great deal of time involved in fund-raising so that I can ensure that the children in our school have all the benefits possible." He is not talking about any small amount; their yearly goal is a minimum of $60,000. Parental involvement in their school has meant that the children have workbooks in which they can write the answers; they have an art teacher, and they have a special resource science teacher, funded entirely through the PTA. Mr. Engel laughs, "Of course, sometimes, it's not always so grand. One year, we bought toilet paper. The school had already used up its allotment before the end of the year. If you're a teacher with a classroom of kids, that becomes quite a problem, but it's one that the teacher shouldn't have to worry about."

In addition to the monetary support, the Dads' Club has done some of the heavy janitorial work that needs to be done, they've put on a Dads and Daughters Night, a Dads and Sons Night, and they've donated construction skills to build things that the school could use.

"Let's face it," he says, "how much contact would the average father have with his child's school? The Dads' Club has provided an opportunity to know the principal, to understand the workings of the school better, and to socialize with other fathers concerned about education." He admits that it's sometimes a pain to work another meeting into an already crowded schedule, but he adds, "Look what we're accomplishing!"

Laurie Ringel is a Deerfield, Illinois, mother with three sons under the age of eleven. She got very involved in her school's PTA because she believes that while faculties, administrators, and school boards look at education as a whole, the PTA can zero in on individual needs that are important. For example, she says, "The Board of Education didn't think that playgrounds were a high priority. We did. We felt it would give the children a valuable physical outlet, so we raised the money and installed the equipment we felt was needed.

"My being involved in the PTA has had direct benefits for my children. For example, we decided to create an after-school activities session. The school gave us permission to use the facility, we raised the funding to pay for materials and teachers; we decided what to offer, and then we interviewed and hired the teachers to teach the classes. We gave the kids the opportunity to extend their education to horizons beyond those available during regular class time, such as calligraphy, woodworking, and karate. I put a lot of work into this program, but it paid off in many ways. There was the thrill of watching lots of children excited about learning new skills. On a personal level, my oldest son took woodworking, something he would have probably never otherwise been exposed to, and he loved it. He has real ability in this area, and it was an exciting discovery. One of my younger sons took karate. The teacher we hired was from quite a distance away, and it would have been much too far for me to take my son to him for lessons. By joining together and creating a class at the school, we were able to bring the best to us."

During Mrs. Ringel's involvement with the PTA, she feels two even greater goods were accomplished. "People sometimes say that parents are deluding themselves if they feel that they're really that important to the school system, but I'll never believe that argument after knowing what a group of us were able to do for our kids.

"The school board had made the decision that a school in our district would have to be closed, and it looked as if it were going to be Wilmot which was the school my children attended. We parents at Wilmot were quite upset at the thought of our children having to leave their neighborhood school, so we banded together and vowed to research every aspect to see if there wasn't justification for keeping our school open. We did a detailed comparison of every feature of our school and the other school that could be closed instead. We even went in and measured the physical size of each classroom in both schools. We evaluated the art and music space; we showed that our school had a gym/stage combination that could be used for many purposes. We never denigrated the other school; we just showed every positive point about our school. When we finished, the school board was impressed. They thanked us for our efforts and admitted that they'd have never had the time nor the manpower to complete all the statistics we'd presented. Ultimately, even though their initial leaning had strongly been to close our school, the board reversed itself, closed the other school, and our children were able to stay at their neighborhood school."

Mrs. Ringel was also involved in a group that suspected asbestos in the ceilings and pushed to get it measured and taken care of immediately. "I'm sure that it would have happened anyway," she concedes, "but I think we significantly speeded the process of protecting our children's health."

Charla Wilbur, a Littleton, Colorado, mother has an eighth-grade daughter and a son who is a senior in high school. The junior high in her area opened five years ago, and she has been a vital part of the parent group through both her son's and daughter's junior high years. Also active during her children's elementary schooling, she says, "There is a tremendous drop-off in parent interest and participation after their children leave elementary school." Why? Mrs. Wilbur suspects two reasons. She thinks that burnout accounts for some of the problem. Parents who were very active when their children were younger see all the parent sign-up information come home from junior high and high school and think they've been this route before and they've had enough. There's also the mistaken parental belief that now that their children are older, parents are not needed at school. Certainly most teenagers reinforce those feelings. It's a wonderful feeling when a parent walks into his first grader's classroom and the child's face lights up. Whatever the parent had to cancel to get there seems worth it. However, in junior high or high school, the visit may be greeted by having the child slink down in his seat and pretend he doesn't know the parent. Understandably, the parent may wonder why he is bothering. Ironically, that's just the time that Mrs. Wilbur feels you most need to be there. "We're sensitive to a thirteen-year-old's easy embarrassment level, and that's why we work behind the scenes, but believe me, it's well worth it to still be involved. In addition to the good you do for the educational system, you do a lot to help yourself in terms of parenting successfully during your child's teenage years."

She speaks of her PCO (Parent Community Organization) planning and putting on a number of parties for the twelve- to fourteen-year-olds. "As they begin socializing, we want them to see that there are lots of ways to have a good party without drugs and without alcohol. We're not only giving them a place to go and something to do with their friends, but we try to make the parties really special so that our message will be clear in the kids' minds."

Like millions of other American parents concerned about kids' potential substance use and abuse, Mrs. Wilbur worked with the PCO to bring drug-education sessions into the school for parents and kids. "We had the paramedics and the sheriff's department come to school in the evening to talk to parents about what was happening right here in our community. The program was an eye-opening

success. So often, it's easy to say those things might happen elsewhere, but they couldn't take place here. Sessions like ours give
parents a common ground for further discussion and for holding
the line firm when their own children say that everyone else is doing
it."

Though they don't work in their own children's classrooms,
many PCO parents do work at the school as volunteers. They work
with the counseling staff in helping to do paperwork and filing so
that overburdened counselors with already high ratios can spend
their time working with kids. They work in the attendance office
manning phones to call the home of every child who is absent. "That
helps discourage truancy and provides a sense that someone cares
whether that child is in school." Mrs. Wilbur says that the seemingly
simple task of calling on absentees is actually improving education
for everyone in the school since good attendance is necessary for
improved learning. "If a teacher has seven to ten kids absent every
day, she must spend much of her time giving makeup work; thus
by encouraging good attendance, I'm helping make sure my kids
can spend their classroom time on new learning." This easy task of
calling absentees is only one example of the many things parents
do, but it, like most of their activities, is getting the desired results
as well as giving involved parents a chance to know what's really
happening at school.

"As kids get older, we don't want them to think it's uncool to
care about school. By staying involved as parents, we are not just
telling our children that they should go to school and do well; we're
showing them that school is still a very important place. Even more
significantly, perhaps, we are keeping the lines of communication
open at just the time when kids begin to close them off. What better
payback could any parent ask for?"

As a teacher and a parent, I agree with Mrs. Wilbur. The family is
critical to establishing the best learning environment for a child. If
there is no continuity between the classroom and the home, your
child loses an important source of support. School and life become
two separate things, and school learning gets left behind with the
three o'clock bell.

RECENT RESULTS OF PARENTAL INVOLVEMENT

It isn't just me or these four very involved parents who've found that being a part of their children's school makes a difference. Every recent study done validates the importance of a parent's interest and involvement in his children's education. There are far too many to even begin to list, but here are the results of several. Taken in different places by different groups, using students from different backgrounds and socioeconomic status, the results speak for themselves.

- An inner-city New Haven elementary school wanted to improve the quality of student learning. It began by developing school committees with elected parent representatives. These committees evaluated programs and helped in selection of staff and curriculum. In addition, parents were recruited and trained as parent-aides and began regularly working in the classrooms.

  Begun in 1968, the program boasted quite a rate of success by 1975 when students at the school ranked ahead of all other inner-city schools in reading and math skills. They had moved from twentieth in reading and thirty-first in math to tenth place in both among all the schools in New Haven.*

- In Michigan three school districts worked on improving reading scores of their students. In all three districts parent participation was built into the program. However, in the first district it consisted of a community information program of at least four informational meetings a year. The second district had an open house at the beginning of the year and a demonstration at one PTA meeting of the reading program. The third district had in-service training programs for teachers, administrators, and parents. Forty parent leaders were trained, and they in turn conducted workshops for other parents. Also, parents and schools involved

---

* James P. Comer, *School Power* (New York: Macmillan, The Free Press, 1980).

in this district received vouchers redeemable for educational materials.

Reading improved in all three districts; however, students in the third district scored significantly higher than the other two. Why? Researchers found that the programs were virtually the same except for the increased involvement of the parents in the third district.*

- A national study included twenty public high schools in eight states and involved over 20,000 students, 1,000 faculty members, and 20 principals to find out what was important to creating academic achievement and high student aspiration. The result: Parental and community interest in quality education was the most critical factor in both areas. Students of basically the same ability and family educational background did better in math achievement and more often aspired to college when they were the children of parents who were involved in the high school. †

- High school students were asked to report their approximate grade averages, and those grades were compared to parent involvement. The National Center for Education Statistics showed that students receiving mostly A's had the greatest percentage of parents who almost always knew the child's whereabouts, of parents who talked to their children almost every day, of parents who attended PTA meetings, and of a mother and father who kept close track of how well the child did in school. As the grades reported got lower and lower so did the percentage of parents who were involved.‡

---

* Ronald M. Gillum, "The Effects of Parent Involvement on Student Achievement in Three Michigan Performance Contracting Programs" (Paper presented at AERA annual meeting, New York, April 1977 ED [ERIC Document] 144 007).

† Edward L. McDill, Leo Rigsby, Edmond Meyers, "Educational Climates of High Schools: Their Effects and Sources" (Johns Hopkins University Center for the Study of Social Organization of Schools, Baltimore, April 1969, ED 030 205).

‡ *Network,* National Committee for Citizens in Education, September 1985.

WHAT IF YOUR CHILD'S SCHOOL DOESN'T WANT YOUR HELP?

Maybe all of these facts, figures, and personal stories of success have motivated you to become more active in your child's school. If so, that's terrific, but consider this cautionary note. The proof that active parents create better schools does not necessarily mean that you will be excitedly welcomed by the school staff. Why not? Most parents don't stop to think that as much as they feel intimidated by tackling the school system, so do teachers feel threatened by parent involvement.

Of course, every school will say it welcomes parent interest, but to some schools that simply means, "Care about what your child is doing; come to the school functions we offer for families." You may encounter real resistance as you ask to serve on substantive committees, want to make changes in the school, or ask to begin a volunteer parent-aide program.

That doesn't mean you should give up on your school, but it does mean you should proceed with some sensitivity. For example, I believe that parents working in the classroom is a situation that mutually benefits parents and teachers. The parent gets a good understanding of his child's learning and the teacher gets good assistance. So why do many teachers resist it?

Consider that for many teachers their last twenty contacts with parents may all have been to discuss problems about children. Very infrequently do teachers hear when a child went home excited about a project, or about the momentary pride a parent felt when a child was able to read something formerly too difficult. So to many teachers, the thought of having a parent in their classrooms is immediately negative. They see their every move being questioned and their every comment having to be justified. In short, the teacher feels that the parent looms as an intimidating presence that she simply doesn't need.

The parent, of course, sees things a little differently. He hears that his child's teacher won't allow parents in the classroom, and he assumes that the child has a poor teacher who is trying to hide something. Let me stress that is not necessarily the case. Some of the best teachers I know are terrified of having you in their classroom.

If you encounter this type of resistance in your school, it doesn't mean you should give up on the idea of parents in the classroom. It simply means that you'll have to demonstrate how valuable having your help would be. Begin by having the parent group suggest to teachers that they'd like to help out in the classroom, and list some of the benefits of such an involvement. "We could grade workbooks and tests and record them, we could run off assignment sheets, we could give makeup tests, and we could do typing." Work through the parent group to find a teacher who is willing to give this a try. Carefully train the parents who will participate. Stress the following rules:

- Parents must show up when they say they will. If a teacher is counting on the parent to get certain tasks done, and the parent fails to arrive, the teacher is left with more work than she would have had if she'd never counted on the parent in the first place.

- Parents must not try to use the time they are there for personal conferences with the teachers. It isn't worth it to have a parent grade papers for a half hour and then buttonhole the teacher for the next hour for a conference about her child. Of course that doesn't mean that the parent shouldn't request a conference whenever she feels she needs one, but she shouldn't expect the payoff for each week of help she offers to be a personal conference about her child.

I don't believe that any teacher should have classroom parental help forced on him. If the parent group can find a teacher or two willing to try, and the parents adhere to the rules listed above, the teachers who use parent-aides will become the group's biggest advocates. It will be those teachers who marvel in the faculty workroom at how they have fewer papers to grade and more time for individualized work with children in the classroom.

Once you have established parents in the classroom as a good thing for teachers, the next hurdle is getting enough parent involvement. Parents are concerned that they will feel stupid, or be asked to do tasks they either can't or really don't want to do. Thus, it's important to gear your program so that parents can fill out a card saying what types of work they'd like to do and if there are any things they'd prefer not to do. These cards should be given to the teachers, and teachers should be aware that parents have been promised that they would not have to do anything which they'd requested not to do. For example, a woman whose sixth-grade son was a math whiz requested that she not have to be involved in any way with helping students in math. "I don't want my son to know how weak my own skills are." However, she was perfectly comfortable typing tests or running them off for the teacher.

Good communication is the key to effective parental involvement. In any school where there is an attitude that everyone is working together to try to help the student achieve, the climate is such that almost anything can be accomplished.

HOW TO ACTIVATE PARENTS
AT YOUR CHILD'S SCHOOL

How can you get involved? Check first with your school to see what types of groups and programs already exist. Chances are the school has some sort of parents' group. If not, you may need to be the one to get such a group started. Make an appointment with the principal and see if you can design and distribute flyers to be sent home with each student. On the flyers designate a date, time, and place for a meeting of those interested in forming a parents' group. Use those who attend as the core of a group and continue to try to get more people involved. Though it may seem like more work, you'll want to get as many people involved as possible, and don't forget teachers. If you're all working toward common goals of excellence in education, why leave them out? Once a parent-teacher group has been established, it can become a valuable source of informal communication.

Perhaps the largest and the most commonly known membership parent group in the United States is the PTA or Parent Teacher Association which has 5.6 million members in 24,000 schools. Almost everyone has heard of the PTA, but to many parents its actual workings are rather vague. One fact which is not commonly known is that PTA membership is open to everyone; you need not have a child in school to belong. In the last few years, the national PTA has worked with the March of Dimes in developing programs to help parents communicate better with their children in order to reduce the number of teen pregnancies. The PTA has worked on education projects to prevent drug and alcohol abuse, promoted the use of seat belts for children, and developed programs to address latchkey kids. The national PTA offers various incentive awards to provide interest and recognition to outstanding local programs which include an Educator of the Year Award to recognize an inspirational teacher, and a reading award that recognizes a local PTA which has planned effective projects to help parents help their children become readers.

At some schools the parents have decided to eschew national affiliation and have developed a local parent group that they feel better meets their needs. Either way, these groups can provide you with a way to keep informed about what's happening in your child's school, to have an impact on the school staff and programs, and to provide a forum in which to share information and solutions to parenting problems.

If you feel that parents could be doing more at your school, but you're not sure what, consider checking these resources.

- *Your School: How Well Is It Working?* This booklet, put out by the National Committee for Citizens in Education, talks about what qualities exist in a good school, how to evaluate your school, what traps to avoid in evaluation, and what strategies exist to improve schools.

- *Looking in on Your School, a Workbook for Improving Public Education.* This workbook, put out by the national PTA, provides specific questions for you to ask about the goals of the school, the administration, the teachers, the students, the curriculum, the support services, the library, the school plant, school financing, the parents, and the community. Space is provided next to each question for compiling the answers you receive and action suggestions follow each group of questions.

- *Beyond the Bake Sale, an Educator's Guide to Working with Parents,* Anne T. Henderson, Carl L. Marburger, Theodora Ooms. This book, available from the National Committee for Citizens in Education, gives many specific suggestions for involving parents as problem solvers and decision makers within the school. It provides examples of successful policies that create more home-school collaboration. Although it is primarily geared toward educators, parents may find it interesting reading since it challenges, "Think of parents as your partners in education. You must and can involve all parents so that they will directly support and reinforce their child's learning."

- *Parent Participation and Student Achievement: The Evidence Grows,* edited by Anne Henderson and put out by the National Committee for Citizens in Education. This resource booklet provides an annotated bibliography of recent research on parent participation. Not only do the brief reviews provide interesting reading, but they give further concrete evidence to the fact that parental involvement does make a big difference in student success. PTA and PTO groups may find the studies helpful in convincing more parents to participate in their child's education.

WHAT ABOUT WORKING MOMS ALREADY STRETCHED TO THE LIMIT?

I realize that today's families are busier than ever, and in many cases both parents work or the parents are divorced and Mom already feels as if she's trying to be Superwoman. As the working mother of two children myself, I know that these parent-participation suggestions could seem intimidating to impossible. "Where," you might think, "am I ever going to begin to get the time or the energy to get involved in the schools in the way this chapter suggests? I'm lucky to figure out how to get everyone fed, and to bed at a decent time." The answer is although it is certainly worthwhile to do as much as you possibly can at your child's school, you shouldn't feel guilty if you have limitations that keep you from being as active as you'd like. Even if your involvement in your child's school does not go beyond reading the newsletters to stay apprised of what is happening, making certain that you see the work your child is doing, looking at the papers that have been returned to him, and sharing interesting elements of your work and life that relate to school activities, you will be doing a great deal to help him be more successful in his school years. If you make your child feel that school is an important place in your eyes and that what goes on there extends beyond the classroom, you will be providing an excellent pathway for him to follow on the road to a good education.

THREE

COMMUNICATING WITH YOUR CHILD

"Hi, son, glad you're home. How was school today?"

"Fine."

"What did you do?"

"Nothing."

This classic conversation has taken place in so many families for so many years that it evokes smiles among almost all parents. The problem it delineates, however, is not so funny. Parents know that it's important to talk to their children about school, but they don't know how to get their children to talk to them.

WHY WON'T MY CHILD TALK TO ME?

While it's important to establish a good rapport with your children, that doesn't mean that you need nonstop patter. Some children are by personality much more inclined to talk than others. They enjoy going through the whole day bit by bit, telling you who got whom out in four square, how many times they got called upon to speak in class, and which items from their lunch that they chose to trade with a friend. Other children would not turn up with such detailed information even if they were grilled relentlessly. As one mother explained, "For several years I felt like such a failure. My neighbor's child and mine were in the same class and my neighbor's daughter told her mother everything. I felt like I must be doing something wrong as a mother because my daughter didn't want to communicate with me. Then my second child started school. She couldn't wait to give the details of the day. I realized I hadn't done anything differently; my children just had different personalities."

That's an important factor to remember. Actually, I don't think it matters whether your child gives you every detail of his school day *as long as he feels that he can come to you whenever he does have something that he's concerned about.*

Of course, there are some things you can do to facilitate communication and to encourage your child's comments. When do you attempt to have conversation with your family? Forget pinning your child down as soon as he comes home from school. Think how you feel after you've come home from a day at work. Chances are you want to stretch out and relax, and you don't feel like beginning a detailed recitation of what happened all day. Kids are the same way. They may want to flop down to watch a TV show, go outside to play with a friend, or talk on the phone, but many kids do not want to immediately recount the day they just finished. So begin establishing a good relationship by not hitting the child with questions as soon as he walks in the door.

Dinnertime can be a good time for the family to share aspects of the day, but only if everyone talks and the child doesn't feel as if he's on stage having to recite. Not too long ago, I overheard one student tell another, "Yeah, our dinner conversations are great. My dad grills me about school, but let me ask him about what went on at his office, and he tells me it's none of my concern."

"We don't have those problems," said his friend. "We've got a TV in the kitchen, so we don't have to talk to each other." There's no doubt that having to fit comments into the duration of television commercials does little for effective communication.

MOM, DID YOU HEAR WHAT I SAID?

Listen to your child when he does talk to you. Sometimes that's not easy to do. You have a lot else on your mind, and your child may seem to take the slow route around China to get to the point of what he is saying. The easiest thing to do is to tune out for a while. Kids, though, are pretty smart. They quickly figure it out when you ask them questions and then don't listen to the answers. Soon they quit giving any answers. A simple shrug or "I don't know," becomes their standard response.

Good listening means that you don't keep interrupting with more questions before your child has had a chance to finish expressing his thoughts. You may think you're just pinpointing the information you really want to know, but it's frustrating for the child. He's getting to what he wants to tell you. Of course, that doesn't mean you should never ask your child anything; it just means you shouldn't interrupt him to do so.

CREATING EFFECTIVE CONVERSATION

The other day I listened to a very intelligent mother tell her six-year-old, "Paint a picture of your day for me with your words."

"Well," said the little girl, wrinkling her forehead in thought, "it was blue."

"Blue," said the mother, trying not to show her concern over the fact that blue often symbolized loneliness or depression. "That's very interesting. What other colors was your day?"

"Just blue," replied the child. Then she looked at her mother. "Every day you ask me that. What color do you want it to be?"

There is a definite value in trying not to read too much into every conversation, but when you do begin a conversation with your child try to ask questions that are starters instead of enders. Did you have a good day? Uh huh. Do you have any homework? No. Did you have a test today? Huh uh. You get the general idea of why such questions don't work. You either end up like a police sergeant barking further questions or the conversation ends. Avoid yes-no types of questions and instead, try asking open-ended ones that give the child the potential of further explanation. One mother said, "Every so often, I try something really off the wall, and it usually works. This was our conversation last night. I started by saying, 'So who fell down on the playground today?"

"Allan," answered her startled son. "He fell off the climbing bars. How'd you find out about it?"

"I just guessed," replied the woman. (It seemed a pretty good bet that some child in the elementary school might have fallen down during the course of a normal school day.) "So what did the nurse say about him?"

"Oh, he didn't go to the nurse. Right after recess we have spelling, and we were having this huge test, and he didn't want to miss it."

"I remember spelling tests in school. Some words were always a lot harder than others. Some I could remember right away, and others took forever."

"Yeah," said the child, "that's how it is for me too. Especially with the word 'appear.' I always get it wrong. Math is a lot easier than spelling."

"How come?"

"I think it's because Mr. Griffith is so nice. He always answers our questions, and he makes us laugh."

"I like Mr. Griffith, and he says you work very hard in his class. I'm really proud of that. Maybe I could review your spelling words with you at home."

It's amazing how much was revealed from the beginning of a seemingly innocuous conversation. If you don't enter the conversation with a preconceived mind set, you may learn far more from your child.

Sometimes bedtime can be a good time to talk to your child about school. One mother says that she sits on the edge of her nine-year-old's bed, turns the lights down low, and goes through a poem they've done together since he's been three. Then she asks him to tell her a little about his day. Relaxed and ready to drift off to sleep, he frequently shares more in-depth kinds of feelings than he would be willing to risk during the day.

When conversation is best depends on your particular family's schedules and personalities. The important thing is that you have some quality time built in in which you have the best chance of establishing meaningful conversation. Prevent "How was school?" from becoming as routine as "How are you?"

Try to listen as nonjudgmentally as you can and to interrupt only with comments that encourage more conversation. For example, suppose your child says, "Sally came to school with her hair dyed green yesterday."

Do you say, "That's stupid. You better never do that to your hair"?

If so, chances are your child will become defensive or close off the conversation, so let's try the dialogue again. Your child says, "Sally came to school with her hair dyed green yesterday."

You reply, "Oh, what'd you think of it?" This allows your child to continue the conversation, and you to get a lot more insight into why your child brought the matter up and what she is thinking about it. That doesn't mean that you have to allow her to dye her hair green. In fact, it's important to note that communicating effectively with your child doesn't mean that you have to give up your principles; it just means that if you listen before you speak, you may find out a great deal more that's important to know. It's fine to have certain standards and expectations and to let them be known. In my years in education, I've found that parents who try above all else to be friends with their children usually have children who are real discipline problems.

BELIEVE IN YOURSELF AS A PARENT

While it's very important to make your child feel as if your home is a loving, accepting one in which he can and does talk freely, it's an unrealistic burden to put on yourself to expect that there will never be tension or discord or that every conversation with your child will be meaningful. As parents we are not perfect. To expect it of ourselves only leaves us feeling frustrated and angry.

Sometimes we are going to say or do the wrong thing, and the world won't end; our children will not stop loving us. Yet we can at least attempt to follow the rules of good communication. A genuine interest that shows, eye contact, and a nod or a noncommittal response that encourages further explanation are bound to get a better response from a child.

Remember that you've got a great deal to offer your child. One of the most haunting memories I've had since I've been teaching revolves around a fourteen-year-old named Cindy and her parents. There was no doubt that Cindy was quite bright and could be quite a handful. "I'm not reading William Sydney Porter," she announced to the class when I gave the assignment. "His work is stupid and immature."

"Okay," I said. "I'll accept that premise if you want, but only if you prove it. I want you to give me concrete examples from his short stories and reasons that illustrate how his work is stupid and immature."

"What if I don't?" she asked.

"Cindy, since this doesn't involve the whole class, you can see me after class for the consequences, or you can refer to your class-rules sheet about the matter." With that I went on with class, and the next day, I noted that Cindy had read the assignment and was willing to add to the discussion.

From time to time, Cindy tried to push; I didn't give in, but I liked her, and I think she knew it. I watched with growing concern as Cindy first chopped off her lovely long brown hair and then began gaining a great deal of weight. One day, she was absent. Two days later she was still absent, and I received a call from her parents asking if they could come in and talk with me.

They came to school, and we began to talk. Cindy's mother was half frantic. She said that she had come to see me because Cindy had mentioned that she really liked me, and maybe I knew where she was.

I was confused. "Isn't Cindy at home?"

Cindy's mother stifled a sob and said that Cindy had run away from home. "We told the attendance office she was at home. Actually, we don't know where she is, and it's really all our fault."

"I'm sure that's not true," I said, trying to make the parents feel better. "Why do you feel that way?"

"She was always so smart. Her father and I are just ordinary. Why, from the time Cindy's been about eight, she's been smarter than we've been. What was the point of our telling her what to do?"

At once, so many pieces of the puzzle were clear to me. Cindy's hair cutting, her weight gain, her challenging of adults. She was looking for some limitations in her life, some adult guidelines of rules she had to follow. Her parents obviously loved her, but they'd allowed themselves to be totally buffaloed by her. I wanted to tell them that no matter how smart their fourteen-year-old was, they still had years of knowledge that came from the experience of living, and they shouldn't be intimidated by her. Only it was too late for words; Cindy was already gone.

So many parents with whom I deal seem to be bewildered by their children. They're so worried about doing something wrong to damage their children's psyche, they do nothing at all. "I don't want my son to stop talking to me," explained one mother, "so I try not to contradict him."

HANDLING THE HOUSE RULES

I don't believe that effective communication is stifled by the parent clearly establishing that there are certain house rules to be followed, and that there are consequences for not following them. Clear communication can keep many potential problems from ever becoming problems. For example, last year a neighbor's child came home and announced that she was trying out for cheerleader at her school. "I think that's great," exclaimed her mother. "I hope you make the squad. Tell me about tryouts."

The twelve-year-old did and I thought how well this parent-child communication was working. The family was elated when the girl made the cheerleading squad, but not for long. The next time I ran into my neighbor, she complained in front of the girl, "I really want Kim off cheer. You can't imagine how it's disrupting everything. I'm always driving her to practices, to games, to spirit planning meetings, to sign paintings." Kim frowned sullenly.

When Kim first said she wanted to try out for cheerleader, it would have been a good opportunity for her mother to ask what kind of time commitment was necessary. As a school-club sponsor, I've seen kids start projects many times and then announce midway through that they have to drop out because their parents are making them. Not only does this leave the club in a bind and make other students who must pick up the slack angry with their friend, but more importantly, it gives the child who quit at parental urging the message that when commitments get to be too much, you just drop them.

It's great to want your child involved in school, but when he asks you about participating in a particular activity, before you say yes, it might be wise to find out what kinds of things it entails. If he does take part and the commitment turns out to be more than you or he thought it would be, help him through the experience that time and then don't let him do it again.

As you establish the rules in your household, it's important to be consistent, reasonable, and fair. I think of a thirteen-year-old boy named Allan whose self-image suffered greatly from the bowl-shaped home haircuts that his father gave him. One afternoon, I tried to tactfully mention them to the father. He responded, "I don't mind providing the best for my family's education; in fact, I'm buying Allan a computer, but I don't want him to think that money grows on trees for pointless extras like professional haircuts!"

Allan's father only saw the important value he was teaching his child. He never stopped to think that his edict had caused Allan to sink silently in the back of each class so that he never called attention to his hair, and his father never saw the look of anguish on Allan's face when another student called him "bowl-head."

Though you certainly are doing your child no favor if you give into the "but everyone else is doing it . . ." argument, it's important that your rules not be established just to show who's in charge, and that values be taught in a constructive instead of a destructive way.

WHAT DO YOU EXPECT FROM YOUR CHILD?

From the time your child is very small, you communicate your expectations to him, and your feelings make a big difference in what he accomplishes. Most researchers now support the fact that high expectations do a great deal to achieve maximum learning. As parents and educators we must concentrate on what our children can achieve. I often think of the quote by Blake, "What is now proved was only once imagined." Who knows what our children may be able to accomplish if we support their endeavors and feed their curiosity.

That isn't to say that we shouldn't be realistic. We cannot live through our children, nor can we make them some fantasy of what we want them to be. Many of the counselors to whom I spoke complained of this problem. Said one, "I'm trying to talk with a parent about how we can help his child bring his grades up to a C average, but the parent isn't interested in that. He wants to know my opinion about which college would be best for undergraduate studies to make certain his child gets into a good graduate school. What I want to say to the parent is take off the rose-colored glasses, and let's look at reality."

That's not easy to do. All of us want success for our children, and it's difficult to see them objectively. However, just because it doesn't look as if your child is going to be a future Nobel prize-winner doesn't mean you can't be positive and have high expectations for his behavior. All kids can learn. It may take a different strategy; it may take more time, but you should never label your child a failure. People simply do not perform higher than they are expected to perform, and if your child perceives himself as a failure, it will be a self-fulfilling perception.

It's tricky to set expectations for your child that are high but not unrealistic. Even the brightest child will fail if you expect perfection. So how do you know what kinds of expectations you should be setting for your child? If you are feeling uncertain, you might want to talk to your child's teacher, and ask her if she thinks the expectations you have are realistic. It's a temptation, but you should not base your expectations for your child on what your neighbors and friends have established for their children. There are two reasons for this. The first is that your neighbor's child is a different person entirely than yours. He may be the same age, but his strengths and weaknesses may be quite different than your child's. Furthermore, your neighbor or friend may have off-target expectations for her child or a different set of values than you have. If you are really concerned about whether you have valid, realistic expectations for your child, consult with objective experts.

Tied in to having high expectations is the necessity to celebrate your child's achievement. What good is success if there is no sense of joy and reward in having succeeded? In fact, according to Dr. Carol Grosse, an expert who lectures across the country on the topic "Raising Student Expectations, Raising Achievement," the more you concentrate on rewarding success, the less you'll find it necessary to punish misbehavior. Everyone likes praise. Though a parent may start out having to design external kinds of praise, such as an ice-cream cone, an extra half hour before bedtime, or a family game, after a while, parents can begin to turn praise inward by saying such things as, "Lauren, look at that report. I'll bet you're really proud of yourself." In this way the child begins to learn that while it's nice to get others' compliments, the best kinds of feelings come from knowing inside that he's done his best.

It's much easier to start building high expectations from the time a child first enters school than it is to suddenly decide about the time he enters high school that he isn't taking the whole thing very seriously. From an early age children need to be made to feel that learning and school are important. However, academic expectations are not the only ones to be considered. It's also important to let your child know that you expect him to be honest and a good person. The "good" student who taunts a slower classmate or who is willing to cheat to make certain he gets the grade he wants is missing a great deal in the way of an effective education even if he makes straight A's.

Suppose your child does cheat or lie. Obviously, you're not going to be happy about the situation, but probably every child does so at some time in his life. The key is to let him know that it's not acceptable to do such things, without labeling him as a cheater or a liar. If you call him a liar, he has nothing to lose by continuing to lie. If instead, you explain that lying is simply not acceptable in your family, and there are consequences for doing so, you will have gotten across the idea that lying is wrong, without branding the child with a negative image of himself. You've also made him take responsibility for his actions.

Establishing high expectations and good communication will not only help your child be successful in school, but it will teach him valuable skills that he can use throughout his life. Dr. Grosse maintains, "You will have taught your child how to look at his current position, establish high but realistic goals, work to achieve those goals, take time to enjoy and celebrate their completion, and then establish a new set of goals to be met. These are techniques that will allow your child to achieve success in many different areas."

*F*OUR

THE RIGHT STUDY SKILLS: A Key Ingredient to Success in School

By helping your child develop good study skills, you are giving him the incredible gift of maximizing his potential for achievement and minimizing his chance for failure. However, the key to giving your child study guidelines that he will accept and use on a regular basis is in the timing of your suggestions.

Unfortunately, many parents become aware of their children's poor study habits only when a crisis occurs. It's midnight and the paper your child should have finished writing over a week ago is still only half completed. He's rubbing his eyes, yawning, and still trying frantically to write. You're furious that he's put everything off so long, and you feel like letting him know that this is no way to reveal his best work. You want to tell him how terrible his procrastination is, but don't. At that moment he doesn't need a lecture; he, too, wishes more than anything in the world that he hadn't put the assignment off. Of course, that won't stop him from doing the very same thing on the next assignment *unless* you work with him to help him see that procrastination is a major reason that students leave themselves stressed, their parents angry, and their teachers unable to see their best work.

Suppose you approach your child the day after the assignment is turned in and explain the evils of procrastination at that time. You're likely to hear your child say, "I agree with you. It's awful to procrastinate; I never want to put myself through that again. Next time, I'm going to start much earlier." Many parents think that solves the problem and then become very angry with their children when they see the same poor study behavior repeated on the very next project. They can't figure out why their child hasn't learned a lesson, but the answer is simple. Bad habits are hard to change. The remorse is quickly forgotten after the assignment is done, and one heart-to-heart talk isn't enough to make a lasting impression.

To correct unproductive study skills, you, as a concerned parent, will have to show your child how to make changes. It isn't enough just to say, "Don't procrastinate. Start earlier." You'll need to show your child how to set up an organizational chart and a series of deadlines for himself, and you will need to monitor the changes you've suggested until they've become a routine part of his study habits. If your child is young, begin to teach him good study skills while it all seems like part of a game. If he is older and has a number of bad habits, try to approach him in a positive way. Emphasize the fact that you are not criticizing him as a person; you just want to make school easier for him.

You may or may not have help in this effort from your school system. Some schools have begun to implement study skills as part of the classroom instruction, in which case you can help your child by apprising yourself of the school's program and following up on it at home. For example, one elementary school began requiring children to keep a daily calendar in the front of their notebooks and a separate section for each subject. The subject dividers were meant to aid a child in keeping his work organized and readily accessible; the calendar was designed to help a child maintain a daily record of what assignments were due on what dates. Teachers at this school had been instructed to check the children's notebooks once a month to see that they were being maintained correctly, and the principal gave good-notebook awards twice a year. While this program was certainly a step in the right direction, the reinforcement was not frequent enough to ensure an organized notebook. The parent who wanted to make certain these skills were developing might check the notebook weekly or even more frequently. That way the child really would develop the habits necessary for good notebook organization.

In a number of schools, study skills simply are not emphasized very much. Interestingly, in an unscientific poll I conducted of high school students, I found that most of the students felt they'd been given little or no help at any point of their schooling in developing study skills. Perhaps part of the reason is that teachers feel the amount of subject material to be covered precludes anything further than simply telling students to be certain they stay organized and bring the right materials to class. It's hoped that students will somehow pick up the tools of effective study during the presentation of content material.

However, even if your child's school offers little instruction in developing study skills, he needn't suffer. Here are ways you can help to make your child a super student.

GETTING ORGANIZED WITH
THE TOOLS OF THE TRADE

Bobby failed his English test because the teacher said it had to be in blue ink, and he only had pencil. Sandy got a zero on her math assignment because when the teacher said last call for homework, Sandy was still frantically searching the mess in her backpack to find it. Lisa flunked her Spanish quiz because she'd completely forgotten the teacher had said to study for it. Each of these students was bright enough to get a good grade and yet ended up with failure because of lack of organization.

In the sixteen years I've been teaching, not a day has gone by in which I haven't heard about or seen a student whose academic achievement has been impaired by his lack of organizational skills. If you could walk into my classroom for a day and look through my students' notebooks, you could pretty well predict who has the best chance for success. Sure, it's possible for a totally disorganized person to be brilliant, but on the whole, the better organized kids are, the less work they have to do to achieve excellence. Just as a surgeon must have her scalpels, a mechanic his screwdrivers, and a seamstress her scissors, so must a student have his necessary tools. Yet many parents leave this tool-equipping process totally to their child or else they only participate in the fall when school begins and then bow out. Assume that at all times your child needs a notebook with paper and a pencil case equipped both with pens that write and pencils that are sharpened. A set of labeled folders for each subject area will help him keep assignments organized and ready to be checked or turned in when called for. A daily assignment sheet or calendar is a must, and so is the training to learn to fill it in each day to keep track of assignments. Last week, Jody mentioned that she'd spent an hour on the homework I'd assigned. "An hour?" I questioned. "What took so long?"

"Well," her face reddened, "I wrote the grammar assignment on a scrap of paper, and when I got home, I couldn't find the paper. So, I had to call Tiffany, who wasn't home. Then I had to call Linda, who didn't know which pages either but said to call her back if I found out, and then I had to call Courtenay . . ."

"But Courtenay isn't even in this class," I interrupted.

"I know," Jody said, "but Courtenay had Josh's phone number, and he usually gets the assignments right in here. Then I had to call Josh to find out what we were supposed to do. It took quite a while, but I did do the assignment."

As I looked over Jody's paper, I shook my head sadly. It was obvious that the assignment had been done in a rushed fashion, and Jody later admitted as much. Figuring that she'd spent almost an hour just to *get* the assignment, Jody had been sick of doing English homework before she'd ever begun it.

Helping your child establish an organized school pack at the beginning of each year and checking to see that he maintains it can be a terrific aid to improving his lifelong study habits. The use of the assignment calendar mentioned above would have saved Jody an hour of nonproductive homework time.

If you can make keeping an organized notebook second nature to your child from the time he is in elementary school, then these good habits will be firmly in place when he is older. Such organizational skills may seem basic, but they honestly work. Last year, I called in a young man to see me after school at the onset of the second nine-weeks grading period. "Scott," I said, "you've really got ability. You're sabotaging yourself. You can never find your assignments when they're due; you're always frantically looking for paper when I announce a quiz . . ."

He interrupted me, "But I work better that way. It takes too long to sort everything out every day; besides, I've turned everything in. Sometimes, it just takes me a while to find it."

"Humor me," I said. "For the next nine weeks let's try it my way. If it doesn't work any better, I won't bother you again." Finally, he agreed, and two weeks later, he came back in to see me.

"Your method is awful. It takes me twice as long to get everything in the right folder; it wastes time to have to write down assignments when I already know in my brain what I have to do."

"You promised me nine weeks," I replied, "and of course this seems harder, at first. Once you get used to it, it won't seem to take any time at all."

By the end of the nine weeks, he had to admit that all his teachers had noticed a difference in his work and his attitude, and his grades were improving in both citizenship and academics in every one of his classes. "I'd have never believed it," he said sheepishly, "that something so dumb as getting more organized could have made such a big difference."

THE BEST STUDY SPOT

Your child's homework study spot is his office, and it needs to be as conducive as possible to creating a successful study environment. Perhaps the first thing you'll want to check is where your child is actually studying. Though he may have a desk in his room that has just the right lighting over it, this is not his homework spot if he does the majority of his studying while flopped down on the family-room floor.

If your child is younger, get him in the habit of associating studying with sitting down at his desk. If he's older, and this is already a problem, try this method suggested by a mother who found it a great success. For a week, she said nothing to her son; she only kept a record of where and when she saw him studying. When she did finally approach her son, she got exactly the response she anticipated. "I do study at my desk," he said. "You just happened to catch me at an off-time when I was in front of the TV once." Her son hadn't said this to deliberately lie to her; he honestly believed it.

The mother took out her little sheet. "I didn't want to bug you unnecessarily, so I just kept track for a week. I don't think you realize it, but you've slipped into some real negative study habits. From now on, you're going to have to make sure you get to your desk to get your studying done."

Her approach worked well. She hadn't had to argue, cajole, or threaten her son. The facts were simply and indisputably there in black and white. After seeing the paper, he agreed with his mother that it would be best if the television simply stayed off until all his homework was finished. That way he wouldn't be tempted to stop and watch it as he was walking through the room on a study break.

Not too long ago, I listened to a high school counselor talk to a group of freshmen students about doing well in high school, and his words about a homework station stayed with me. "If you want to make yourself do your homework when you'd really rather do something else, here's a trick that will help. Surround yourself with every possible object and condition that will help you focus on doing your homework, and avoid anything that will direct your attention away from the task at hand."

As you evaluate your child's study area, look for the following:

- a clear, uncluttered space for homework
- good lighting

- a comfortable (but not too comfortable) chair
- study tools within easy reach that include a dictionary, thesaurus, ruler, pencils, pens, and paper

Finally, make sure that your child is nowhere near a television set when he is supposed to be studying. Research shows a marked drop even in mentally gifted elementary education children after just three weeks of intense TV viewing.* And a California study of 500,000 students in sixth and twelfth grades noted a strong statistical relationship between TV viewing and low achievement.† Yet in spite of study after study that shows negative results of too much TV watching, the average set is on seven hours a day, and children in the two-to-five age group spend 27.9 hours each week watching television.‡ That means that the average kindergarten graduate has already seen more than seven thousand hours of television in his lifetime.

Regardless of how much your child tells you that he studies better with the television on, you should insist that it remain off while he is doing his studying. Other than the testimonials from teens, I've never been able to find any research that supports increased learning taking place in front of a television set.

WHAT KIND OF STUDY SCHEDULE?

Homework can't defeat your child if you help him stay on top of his assignments. Each day he should get in the habit of looking over all his assignments before he begins any of them and estimate how much time each will take. Then he should set up a schedule of what he plans to have done by what time.

---

* "What Is Television Doing to Real People?" Joel Swerdlow, *Today's Education,* September-October 1981, p. 60.

† Marie Winn, *The Plug-In Drug: Television, Children, and the Family* (New York: Viking, 1985), p. 80.

‡ Ibid., pp. X, 4.

Speaking of time, it's important to have a specific time set aside every day for study. Work out with your child what that time should be and then try to help him stick to it, so that he is not starting to study just about the time he's falling asleep or you're ready to have the family sit down to dinner. It's important for your child to have a say in setting up when his study time will occur, for ultimately you want him to be responsible for establishing these good habits himself. However, you can encourage and help ensure that the selected time is adhered to by taking extracurricular activities into account in the planning, and by telling your child that you'll tell anyone who calls for him during his homework time that he'll return the call later.

When your child gets long-term assignments, you can help make certain that he approaches them successfully. Teach your child the skill of developing what needs to be done for the long-term project and setting dates by which he'll have everything done. For example, Mrs. Winters was given a note by her daughter's social-studies teacher that the sixth grader had two months to design a creative project dealing with ancient Greece. The child's assignment sheet gave a date by which the project had to be decided upon, and a later date by which the student had to provide a progress report. No doubt the teacher's intentions were to help the student avoid procrastination, and yet, those two checks didn't begin to accomplish all that was needed for the project. Once her daughter had chosen an idea, Mrs. Winters sat down with her daughter and said, "Tell me everything you think you'll need to do for this project."

Because this was her daughter's first time at trying something like this, Mrs. Winters made suggestions and asked questions as her daughter spoke. Finally, when they finished discussing everything that needed to be done, they got out a calendar and used it to put together a timeline to get the work accomplished. Her daughter had decided to make a Trivial Pursuit game of the ancient Greek Olympics and the chart looked something like this:

February 1: Go to school library to get books on Greece
February 2–10: Take notes from the books gotten

February 11: Go to public library (if necessary)
February 12–18: Take notes from new books
February 18: Get supplies
                 (Make a list of what's needed ahead of time)

> *supplies needed:*
>   large white poster board
>   four colors of felt-tip pens
>   index cards
>   rubber cement
>   a game spinner
>   glue

February 18–24: Write questions for category one
February 25–March 2: Write questions for category two
March 2–8: Write questions for category three
March 9–14: Write questions for category four
March 15–18: Make game board
March 19–23: Make playing tokens and rules sheet for game
March 24–28: Finish details of project

By making a flow chart, the child took a gigantic project and put it in manageable terms. Her mother had plenty of time to get the necessary materials for her daughter, and the girl had no last-minute hysterics that she was missing items or that the project was too hard. Everything proceeded smoothly.

In addition to making a flow chart for long-term projects, here are two other study schedule tips that will send your child on the road to success. First, encourage him to study dissimilar subjects in sequence. Material that is somewhat similar can overlap and confuse the mind. If your child shifts his focus entirely, each subject will remain more fixed in his mind. Second, set up a pattern in which there is a study/break, study/break situation. It's good for your child to look forward to a definite time to get up and take a break, and yet to know that he will return to finish his work.

MEMORY TRICKS THAT MAKE STUDYING EASIER

Much of your child's schoolwork involves memorizing material, and for some children this seems to be much easier than for others. From the time your children are small, you can play memory games with them to help them concentrate and learn to remember. For example, there's the old standby, "I'm going to the market and I'm going to get_____." The first person fills in the blank and then every individual after that must repeat what has been said and add an additional item. You can ask your preschooler to remember one or two of the items you'll need at the grocery; you can ask him if he remembers the way to his school and follow the directions he gives you. By letting your child succeed in using his memory from the time he is small, you will have helped him train his mind to make use of his memory in school matters as he gets older.

Over the years, I have found that there are a number of tricks that I can give students to help those of them who have trouble learn to memorize more easily. Here are five different ways you could help your child with memorization skills.

1. Acronyms—Making the first letter of each word or concept to be memorized into a word itself helps a person recall what each part of the word stands for. For example, the nonsense rhyme Wam Jam! might be an easy way to recall: Washington, Adams, Madison, Jefferson, Adams, Monroe; the first six U.S. presidents. Of course, this only works if the names merely need to be remembered, but not necessarily memorized in order.

2. Silly Statements—If you need to remember the presidents' names in the order in which the men were elected, you might try taking the first letter (or more) of each word and putting it in a silly sentence you won't forget. For example: Watch Adam Jefferson Mash Mad Ants, or Wow, A Jumping Monster Meets Mr. Adam. Because these sayings are so silly, they stick in even a reluctant memorizer's mind.

3. Here at Home—Have your child put unfamiliar things into an order with which he is very familiar. For example, most kids can conceptualize walking in the back door of their house and going to their room. Thus, they simply imagine each item connected to the house. For example, you'd say, "Think of George Washington in our laundry room. Try to imagine the picture in your mind. Wouldn't it look silly? How about John Adams in the kitchen, then Thomas Jefferson in the family room, James Madison in the hallway, James Monroe in the bathroom, and John Q. Adams in your bedroom."

By teaching your child to associate an order of items he doesn't know with one he knows well, it becomes much easier to remember the new items.

4. Flashcards—Have your child make a flashcard with each name clearly printed on it. Ask him to look at the name carefully, and say it out loud. Go over it again and again. After he's said the presidents' names aloud several times, ask him to write the words as he says them aloud. By having your child use his voice, his hand, and his mind, he will help himself to remember much better than if he just silently says the items to himself.

5. Rhymes—From the time we are small children, we enjoy hearing things in rhyme. Many of us memorized nursery rhymes without ever trying. Whenever possible a tricky fact that keeps escaping the memory will have a greater chance of being remembered if you can help your child work it into a rhyme. Don't worry about poetic technique. Just come up with something quickly that you think will stick in your child's mind, e.g.:

> Washington, Jefferson, and John Adams went to dine
> Where Madison, Monroe, and J.Q. Adams were in line.

Of course, you can teach your child to make up quick rhymes as I have done in this situation, or in some cases you have only to teach him a rhyme that already exists. Probably you remember learning some traditional school-taught rhymes such as "In fourteen hundred and ninety-two, Columbus sailed the ocean blue," or "When two vowels go a-walking, the first one does the talking."

In addition to these methods there are some techniques that work well in specific types of memorization. For example, I've found that students who have misspelled "congratulations" for years no longer do so after we say that only a RAT wouldn't say cong-RATulations to the winner. In memorizing the material about an author, students who've been having trouble see it much more clearly if we make a chart that lists who, what, where, when, why, and how. It gives structure and order to what may have seemed like a maze of information. Encourage your child not only to use the specific memory devices given above, but also to utilize tricks and techniques that he develops for himself. If learning is a game, it becomes a lot more fun to do.

NOTE TAKING THAT WORKS

Each year I tell my students, "Suppose I could give you a surefire way to have to study less and do better. Who'd be interested?" Almost every hand in the class shoots up, and it's easy to see that the students are eagerly awaiting a magic answer that will suddenly make school easy.

"Pay attention in class, and take good notes," I say.

They look disappointed. "Is that all?" they ask.

"That's it," I reply, "but before you discount it, try something for me for a minute. Imagine that a student has just been absent for a whole week and during that week we've gone over a lot of important material. Suppose I told that student that he'd have to get all the material from a classmate's notes. Whose notes would he choose to use? Look at your notes for the past week. Would he choose yours? Why or why not? Suppose you'd been absent for a week. Whose notes would you want to borrow—what makes those notes good?"

Note taking is a skill that can reduce a student's homework load while increasing his knowledge. Why? Because he is actively involved in learning. The nonnotetaker can daydream while discussion is taking place and miss the material without even realizing it.

In effect, he is hearing the information without ever having to actually process it. The notetaker, however, has to listen to decide what things he wants to write down, and in writing them down, has already begun to implant the information in his mind. Furthermore, if he becomes confused about a point at some later time, he doesn't have to try to remember what he thought he heard the teacher say, because it's all in his notes.

Teachers generally have some sort of organizational basis in presenting their material, and students would do well to give some thought to this when deciding how to organize their notes.

Here are some tips that your child should follow and make part of his normal note-taking habits.

1. Begin each day's notes with both the date and day of the week. This will help keep information in the order it was presented and may even assist in recalling the information on an exam.

2. When taking notes either from a book or from a teacher's lecture, leave a wide margin on one side of the paper. This provides space for questions, comments, or other information that relates to the topic in the notes.

3. Work on getting the main idea from a body of information. No one can take down every single word a teacher says. The child who tries probably processes almost none of the information. Good note taking involves being an active listener, one who can evaluate what is important as he listens. You can help your child develop that habit even by such simple things as having him summarize what happened on the television program he just saw. Can he give you the essence of the plot without recounting it detail by detail or leaving out essential elements that make the story make sense?

4. Get in the habit of a nightly review of the notes taken in class that day. Even the neatest students find that there are moments in which they are in too much of a hurry to write as legibly as

they should. Though at the time a teacher is talking about a particular thing, the notes your child has taken may seem perfectly sufficient, your child may realize by rereading them that night that the notes aren't clear enough. It's still soon enough after the information was given for him to rewrite and revise his notes, but it's been long enough so that he can see what will become trouble spots later on. As he reviews his notes, he may want to underline, circle, or highlight the most important material so that when he goes back to study for a test, all the key points have been emphasized.

CLASS PARTICIPATION

The easiest way to help your child concentrate on the material being taught is to encourage him from the time he starts school to *participate in the class discussions.* If your child is trying to answer the teacher's questions, he is actively processing, questioning, and categorizing the material as it is being presented.

Parental guidance can be a great help in making students believe teachers who say, "There is no such thing as a stupid question." Every teacher who cares about kids welcomes questions, and kids who care about school must be made to understand that asking questions and participating in class is not only their right but an important responsibility.

This message is not always easy to get across. Not too long ago, two students walked into my classroom from their biology class. I couldn't help but eavesdrop on their conversation. "I thought that test was an absolute bear," said one.

"Oh, I don't know. I didn't think it was so bad," replied the other.

"Well, no wonder," said the first, "I mean you're always asking the teacher so many questions in class."

Ironically, the first student still failed to recognize that if he'd asked all those questions, he'd probably be having an easier time on the test as well.

Why don't kids participate more in classroom discussion? They're afraid they'll be laughed at because they've given a wrong answer or asked a foolish question. It's safer to say nothing. To counteract these insecurities, you need, from the time your child first starts school, to help him develop the attitude that it's fine to risk a wrong answer in class. Helping your child establish the habit of getting involved at an early age means that by the time he becomes a teenager and finds everything embarrassing, his class participation skills will already be well set.

One way you can help your child to develop participation in school is to discuss things with him at home. Let him get in the habit of listening to discussion, asking questions, thinking through what others are saying, and formulating answers from the time he is very small.

Aside from embarrassment, students fail to ask questions because they are simply too confused to figure out exactly what to ask. Reassure your child that every teacher who cares about teaching would much rather have a child raise his hand and simply say, "Could you go over that again? I'm lost," than to sit there daydreaming because the material doesn't make sense.

GETTING OUTSIDE HELP

Three days before the final exam, a student came in after school, "I've started reviewing for the test," he said, "and I'm confused. Could you help me?"

"Sure," I replied, "I'm glad you stopped in. Now on what exactly do you want help?"

He fidgeted and looked uncomfortable. "The whole last grammar unit."

We'd spent three and a half weeks on the grammar unit. Over seventeen class days and many assignments had passed. Several times, I'd suggested to him that I thought he needed some extra help and to stop in, but he'd never done so. Now, he was completely confused, and what we might have originally been able to straighten out in a matter of minutes was going to take hours. I was willing to try, but I could see that he was becoming impatient. "I wish," he said, "that I'd come in when I first got confused."

This seems to be a particularly severe problem in math, science, foreign language, and English grammar. Each of these areas relies heavily on an orderly progression of previously learned skills to deal with new content. A student who becomes lost and fails to do anything about it is almost assured of getting more and more confused. After sixteen years of teaching, I can assure you that regardless of academic ability, almost every child's temptation is to put off a possible problem and hope that it will go away. From an educational standpoint, you can help your child a tremendous amount simply by teaching him how important it is to ask for help as soon as he's feeling confused on a particular point. Of course, that doesn't mean he should try to work a math problem one time and if it doesn't come out correctly decide that he needs help. There is a great deal to be learned by trying to work things out for himself. However, if he has stared at a page of geometry proofs for an hour and can't make any sense of it, he should check with the teacher the next day about getting help.

HOW TO HELP YOUR CHILD WITH READING

Billy walked in from school, threw his books on the kitchen table, and announced to his mother that there was no point to his doing any more of his history assignments. "I just quit," he announced. "I gave up watching *The Cosby Show* last night to get my history chapter read, and I still flunked the dumb pop quiz today, so what's the point?"

Billy's concerned mother called his teacher who, at first, seemed skeptical. "You're sure he's really reading the assignment?" The teacher checked the school records and found that Billy's reading skills tested average, and his eyes checked 20/20 vision. She called Billy's mother back. "Why don't you try this. Tonight, after he finishes reading his assignment, you give him a little quiz on the material, and let's see what happens."

Billy's mother did just that, and Billy failed his mother's pop quiz. "I don't understand it," she lamented. "I sat right here in this room with you. I watched you read those pages, and yet you can't answer ten simple questions about them."

The problem? Billy was reading the words, but his mind was a million miles away. He was not concentrating on what he'd read, and consequently, nothing he'd read stayed with him at all. He might as well have been reading the words in a foreign language.

Many systems have been developed to create more effective study reading. The first and best known was developed by Frank Robinson at Ohio State University. He titled his system "SQ3R," and teaching your child to use SQ3R can prepare him to get good information from even the most difficult of texts.

SQ3R

SURVEY—A sneak preview which says to look over all the material before beginning to read any of it. Have your child *read* headings and bold-faced material throughout the material to be covered, *skim* the material in italics, *look* at the graphs and illustrations, and quickly *read* the end of the chapter questions. This whole process should be able to be done in a matter of minutes, and it is well worth the time it takes, for the child now has a good idea of what he's going into before he ever begins the actual reading.

QUESTION—Your child should ask himself, "Having just previewed all this material, what am I supposed to be learning?" If he can answer this question, he is well on his way to success in reading, for he has focused in on what he is doing and has a definite goal.

READ—It is now time for the child to read the material. Because he already knows where the author is going and what the major points are, he should be able to read the material relatively quickly and with good understanding.

RECITE—After your child finishes reading the material, he should take some quick notes on the major points, and then try to say what he's learned.

REVIEW—for a quiz, test, or paper, by going over the material read.

Since Robinson first developed this system, several others have been created with additional steps to them. Walter Pauk, in his book *How to Study in College,* mentions the need for the inclusion of a *reflection* step after the review in which the student "organizes and reorganizes ideas and weaves them into his own knowledge."

I often think of one sophomore English student I had the first year I was teaching. She'd never heard of SQ3R or any other formal method, but she was doing well in my class which had a lot of required reading. One day, she stopped in after school. "I'm so proud of your good grades," I said. "What are you doing that I could pass along to other students? Do you have some special way of reading?"

"I don't think so," she replied. "I mean, I look over the stuff before I actually start reading it, and then when I get finished, I think to myself, "Now, what would Mrs. Fields ask about this?" She smiled. "And I'm usually pretty close to being right."

My experience with this young lady has proven itself again and again over the years. Students who do well have usually figured out something akin to SQ3R method on their own, or they've been helped with it in elementary school. Students who do poorly often read material without any real sense of purpose, organization, or concentration. By helping your child develop effective reading skills, you are giving him an excellent chance for success in school.

Here are a few additional tips to improve reading. If you have an older child who is still reading slowly, you might help him increase his reading speed by suggesting that he stop moving his lips as he reads and that he not point his finger at each word. People can read much faster than they can speak, and their eye movement across the page goes much more quickly if they don't slow it down by pointing.

As your child reads, he should concentrate on reading quickly for main ideas and paying attention to the material being read. If you are concerned about your child's speed or comprehension, check with your school to see what kinds of reading tests and classes are available. Though many parents feel that reading classes stop after elementary school, this is not true. High schools frequently have reading classes too. There are remedial classes for students who need help achieving better comprehension and fluency in their reading, and there are developmental reading classes to prepare students to better read at a college or technical level. Call your child's school; find out exactly what kinds of reading programs are available and what your child has to do to qualify for participation in them.

PREREADING SKILLS

The SQ3R may seem good and well for an older child, but what if your child isn't even in school yet? Is it too early to prepare him to be a good reader? Absolutely not. You can help him develop a healthy attitude toward reading by reading aloud to him and making him excited about learning to read.

Take your child to the library from an early age. Help him to choose some books he'd like to have read to him. In his book, *The Read-Aloud Handbook,* Jim Trelease talks about how regular reading aloud strengthens a child's reading, writing, and speaking. He quotes Courtenay B. Cazden's *Child Language and Education:* "One of the primary learning methods for children is imitation . . . It is this ability to imitate that allows a fifteen-month-old child to say his first words. By the age of two, the average child expands his vocabulary to nearly 300 words and reaches 1600 words by age four. The average adult uses only 1800 different words in his daily vocabulary."

Trelease then asks, "How do you want your child to get that sense of vocabulary, sentence structure, and patterning? It can be from Fred Flintstone and Fonzie or it can be from the books you've taken the time to read to him."

In addition to reading aloud, there are some other games you can play with young children which will aid in enabling them to grasp concepts helpful to reading.

Show your child a box. Ask him to put a ball in the box, over the box, under the box, around the box, behind the box, etc. As he gets good at doing this, speed up and see how fast he can go. You'll be helping him understand prepositions when he learns to read and also to listen carefully for directions.

Help your child write his own book. Let your child tell you a story. Type or print the story he tells you and then read it back to him. This will help your child see the connection between the spoken and written word. You can take this a step further. Cut your child's story and paste some of it on separate pages leaving room for him to draw illustrations at the top. Read the pages to him, and have him help you to put the pages back in sequence.

The importance of reading cannot be overstressed. Statistics show that one in every five Americans is functionally illiterate. We tend to think that such a thing could never happen to our own children, but it can. Stay aware of your child's reading skills. Be encouraging and supportive. As a parent be a role model by showing your child that you read, and if you have concerns that your child is not reading as well as he should be, talk to teachers, ask for special testing, but don't just ignore the matter. Real success in today's schools or society is very difficult without the ability to read.

RECOMMENDED SOURCES FOR GOOD BOOKS

Which book to choose? Standing in a bookstore or library and trying to pick out just the "right" book to keep your child's attention can seem an overwhelming task. Fortunately, there's help from the following sources which recommend books by age and category. Many also give brief plot descriptions. Chances are you can find most of these reference materials in your local library, and while you're there, ask the children's librarian if she has a list of her own favorites for your child's age group.

TO HELP YOU DECIDE WHICH BOOKS TO READ ALOUD

1. *Let's Read Together Books for Family Enjoyment.* Chicago: American Library Association, 1981.

2. Freeman, Judy. *Books Kids Will Sit Still For.* Hagerstown, Maryland: Alleyside Press, 1984.

3. Kimmel, Margaret Mary, and Segel, Elizabeth. *For Reading Out Loud! A Guide to Sharing Books with Children.* New York: Dell, 1984.

4. Trelease, Jim. *The Read-Aloud Handbook.* New York: Penguin Books, 1982, 1985.

TO HELP YOU SELECT BOOKS FOR YOUR CHILD TO READ TO HIMSELF

1. Dreyer, Sharon Spredemann. *The BookFinder. When Kids Need Books.* Circle Pines, Minnesota: American Guidance Service: 3 volumes 1977–1985.

2. Gallo, Donald R., editor. *Books for You, A Booklist for Senior High Students.* Urbana: National Council of Teachers of English, 1985.

3. Monson, Dianne L., editor. *Adventuring With Books, A Booklist for Pre-K-Grade 6.* Urbana: National Council of Teachers of English, 1985.

HELP YOUR CHILD IN MATH

From the time your child is a preschooler, you can help foil math anxiety by playing games with him and letting him use math in everyday situations. Ask him to set the table and then tell you how many pieces of silverware it took. Ask him to watch for stop signs when you are driving and to count how many he sees until you get to your destination. Allow your child to help you make a recipe or let him help you with a simple carpentry task so that he can see the concept of measuring, and experience math in day-to-day situations. Because you've already shown him it's important in the real world, he'll be anxious to learn to add and subtract.

You can help your child learn the meaning of many of the more abstract math vocabulary words by playing this simple game. Get six marbles and a box. Put one marble in the box. Then ask him to put *more* marbles in the box. Have him count the marbles in the box. Ask him whether there are *fewer* marbles in the box than on the counter. Math vocabulary such as *more, less, some, all, none,* can be taught this way. As long as you praise your child when he does well and don't scold when he makes a mistake, he will think the whole thing is a lot of fun.

Every younger child likes to feel important, so let your youngster feel as if he's needed by asking him to count how many people want dessert, how many people want coffee after dinner, etc. In doing this, you are letting the child see a relationship between numbers and objects.

When you take your child shopping, you have a marvelous opportunity to show him the importance of math and how it applies to money. Let the cashier in the grocery store count the change back to him so that he can see different amounts have different meanings. Let him pick out one item each time and show him or let him show you which coins or dollar bills it would take to buy that item.

Kids love to play store. Put price tags on things in your child's room and let him "buy" them from you using real money. You'll be surprised at how fast he can learn to pick out the coins to equal even odd numbers like fifty-nine cents.

Math can be a puzzle that's fun to work, and if your child has this attitude, learning will be easier. You can do a lot to help him with his study skills in math just by giving him the right attitude about learning math.

When he gets into school and begins doing addition, encourage him to make his numbers line up correctly. There are advanced-math high school and college students who can conceptually work very difficult problems, and yet they still receive poor grades because they make simple arithmetic errors due to sloppy number positioning. Think how much harder it is to add a column of numbers when, instead of being neatly written in correct alignment, they're written this way:

$$
\begin{array}{r}
152 \\
421 \\
\underline{36}
\end{array}
$$

Encourage your child from the time that he is young to write neatly and to align his numbers. Whenever you see him do so, praise him, display his papers, and establish a pattern for success in math.

Some tips for making math easier for your child:

1. Math has a logical basis. Therefore, every step in math should be based on a totally understandable reason. Make sure your child understands the reasons for the processes he is performing. If he understands the reasons for his answers, he will be able to figure out similar problems without trouble.

2. Don't tell your child that math was always impossible for you too. One algebra teacher said, "At least half my conferences to discuss a student's problem in a math class begin by a parent telling me how much trouble he or she had with math, so he can certainly empathize with his child's problem. I honestly feel that when parents keep telling a child how difficult something is, the child develops a defeatist attitude that says, 'If Mom or Dad couldn't do this, I probably can't either.'"

3. Most math books from first grade on through higher education contain a sample problem at the beginning of a new assignment. Have your child get in the habit of working through that sample

problem. He should follow the process through once in the book and then close the book and try to work that same problem on his own. That way, if he gets in trouble, he will have a detailed, step-by-step analysis of how to correct his errors. In a way, it's like having a tutor on almost every page of the math book.

4. Do not encourage your child to rely totally on a calculator. Most math teachers feel that calculators are fine once a child has mastered the basics on his own. "It's a scary thought," mused a sixth-grade math teacher, "to think that if his batteries die, a child can no longer add."

HOW TO HELP YOUR CHILD WITH WRITING

This critical skill is growing in importance as America becomes a society in which almost every job involves some degree of clear writing. Over my many years in education, I've found that while most parents accept the need for their children to practice math facts or to spend time memorizing foreign language conjugations, they frequently believe that writing is just a matter of talent and cannot be learned. I must disagree. My students have won hundreds of writing awards, and the key element is not natural talent. That helps, but any child can be turned into a reasonably good writer. To do so, he must practice the skill just as he would drilling math facts or memorizing the conjugation of *hablar*. You can help him develop writing skill from the time he is little. Encourage his creativity and sense of plot development by telling him the beginning of a story and letting him tell you the ending. Become a family pen pal. Let your child write you a question each night which you answer and reply with a question for him. Put together a family newsletter to send at holiday time, but let your child write part of it. Again, from an early age, let him see that writing is an entertaining and effective means of communication.

Most writing teachers find that students spend a tremendous amount of homework time deciding what to write. This is nonproductive, and no student should spend time staring at a blank paper. Instead, encourage your child to brainstorm. If he has been given a topic, he should put it at the top of his paper, and then write down absolutely everything that comes into his mind about it. The items needn't go together, nor must they be in any order. For example, here are two student papers that illustrate brainstorming the very general assignment: Write an essay about cigarette smoking. The students had been given three minutes to write everything that came into their minds about the subject.

- advertising makes it look cool
- more adults are quitting
- more teenagers than ever are starting
- the Virginia Slims tennis tournament
- smokeless tobacco
- why I want to smoke

- "You've come a long way baby"
- death and lung cancer
- my two best friends smoke
- my mother quit smoking after her father died
- the cost of cigarettes
- why do we subsidize cancer research and tobacco farmers
- the time I tried smoking
- smoking in bed can cause fires

Obviously, neither student can use all these ideas. He will have to sort through them and decide which he wants to focus on and which go together. However, he is in the enviable position of having too much material instead of feeling that there is nothing about which to write.

If the student hasn't been given any topic, he should simply choose a nearby item, or a sentence from a newspaper or magazine and begin brainstorming about that. If he's writing, he's producing. Staring at a blank sheet of paper trying to decide on the perfect topic is a frustrating waste of time. If he hasn't learned it at school, you can get your child comfortable with brainstorming by making it a family activity and seeing what each person writes down about different topics. For example, on the following page is one family's brainstormed answers to the word "chair," along with the possible stories and essays that could be written from their responses.

Mom's thoughts

- Chair
- A place to relax
- I need new ones for the kitchen table
- There's nothing in the house for dinner
- I hate grocery shopping
- The stores are so crowded
- I've got too little time and too much to do
- Time like watches
- Kids and Swatch watches
- Fads come and go
- Who gets left out?
- Kids can be cruel

Possible essay topics from these thoughts:

- How to Organize Your Time Better
- A humorous essay on fads
- Why Kids Are Cruel to Each Other

Possible short story ideas from these thoughts:

- A boy steals a fad watch he wants but doesn't have the money to buy. What will happen to him?
- A mother is grocery shopping with her child when her child sees an elf on a cereal box come alive.
- A boy who has been left out of a party vows to get even.

Dad's thoughts

- Chair
- Something you sit on
- My feet are tired
- They hurt when I stand too long, but not when I walk

- They never hurt on a golf course
- I have to fix my slice
- I enjoy golf
- I like parties
- I don't like being alone

Possible essay topics from these thoughts:

- Persuasive essay on why golf is a good sport
- What Makes a Party Fun
- Why People are Lonely

Possible short story topics from these thoughts:

- Two friends are tied for first place in a golf game. One sees the other cheat. What should he do?
- A girl invites everyone to a party, but finds after the people come that she isn't having any fun. Why?
- A man has a strong urge to begin walking. He lets his feet carry him where they may, and suddenly, he realizes that something has happened. He's no longer on earth.

Seventh-grade child's thoughts

- Chair
- My chair is orange
- Oranges are my favorite fruit
- Fruit of the Loom underwear
- Clothes make people happy
- Guess clothes make me happy
- Conjecture
- Teachers like vocabulary words like that
- School—the best thing is plays
- Memorizing lines, doing big musicals
- The fat clown in *Barnum*
- Ronald McDonald

Possible essay topics from these thoughts:

- How Colors Affect People
- Why It Gives People Confidence to Wear Clothes They Like
- How to Try Out for a Play

Possible short story ideas from these thoughts:

- A girl gets the lead in the school musical, but can't seem to memorize her lines.
- A boy cheats on a vocabulary test and the teacher catches him. He has a plan to convince her he shouldn't get punished.
- A girl doesn't get the lead in the school musical after she counted on it. Instead, she gets the part of the fat clown. Will she drop out or take the part?

Third-grade child's thoughts

- Chair
- Rhymes with bear
- He lives in a cave
- Rhymes with a hair that grows on your head
- Rhymes with tear which is what you do with paper
- Write on paper
- Write on napkins
- Write on your hand and get in trouble

Possible essay topics from these thoughts:

- All About Bears
- Why You Should Write Neatly on Your Paper
- Why I Want to Wear My Hair This Way

Possible short story ideas from these thoughts:

- Two boys get lost and wander into a cave. They get inside and hear a bear roar.
- A girl starts talking in rhymes and can't stop.
- A father writes an important message on a napkin and his son accidentally throws it away.

The next step in successful writing is for your child to make an outline of what he wants to say. For an essay he will want to make an outline that looks something like this:

I. Introduction and main idea of the paper
II. Support Statement for main idea

      A. detail about support
      B. detail about support
  III. Support Statement for main idea
      A. detail about support
      B. detail about support
  IV. Conclusion

The level of sophistication of the outline will vary greatly with the age of your child. However, even a very simple outline for a young child helps him see that thoughts need to be organized into some pattern, and that everything he says should have a relationship to the main topic.

The next step is to have the child actually write the paper. That is no longer the impossible task that it once looked. He already has his topic, his ideas, and some way to organize them. He should write a first draft with the knowledge that it can be changed if he doesn't like it, so it doesn't have to be perfect. In fact, this may well be the greatest help a parent can give his child—to encourage him that it's perfectly fine to rewrite a paper. So many children have the idea that if the paper doesn't turn out well the first time, they simply can't write. Rewriting should be presented as an exciting opportunity to play with and change the words until the child has them in just the way they sound best. Adding material, cutting material, and reordering material are very important steps in producing finished quality writing. *The point is that a paper doesn't have to be perfect the first time.* Once your child believes that, he'll feel much less pressure and enjoy writing much more. After he's finished writing the first draft, let him mark all over it, let him cut and paste if he wants to move things around, and finally, encourage him to write another draft. By helping your child build time in his study schedule for writing several drafts of a paper with some lapse between each draft, you'll see that he will improve his writing greatly even without comments or criticism from others.

In addition to helping him develop the right skills in approaching the writing process, you can also improve your child's ability to write by showing him examples of good writing and by showing him the ways writing is applied to the "real world." If writing is a part of your daily job, show your child some examples of why it is important. No matter how frequently English teachers tell students that writing is important, they become much more convinced by hearing it from people in other jobs. One teacher became so frustrated that he finally assigned his students to survey people in other occupations. Terry O. Phelps reports in a March 1986 article in *English Journal* (p. 81) that every one of the ninety-six surveyed occupations required writing, even a head cocktail-waitress position, a truck driver, and a tailor. Phelps's students were amazed to discover that there was writing involved in almost every job and concluded that people are concerned about their writing skills because they don't get enough practice.

If all this information about study skills seems a little overwhelming, remember that you do not have to teach your child every tip in a single night. Merely by watching his study habits and being aware of what constitutes good study skills, you can help your child overcome particular weaknesses that are preventing his best performance in school.

*F*IVE

HOMEWORK: Your Child's Assignments or Your Headaches?

The cartoon is classic. A frustrated parent is poring over his son's or daughter's books and papers. The parent's sleeves are rolled up, sweat is pouring from his brow, and in the background his child is seen outside, playing. "Dad," says the caption, "aren't you finished with my homework yet?"

Of course, this cartoon is an exaggeration of a situation, but perhaps it is not so farfetched as we'd like to believe. Some variation of this cartoon appears at the start of almost every school year, and it seems to touch a chord in parents everywhere. Why? Maybe it's because homework can easily become a source of great frustration and fighting within a family. In this chapter, we'll look at how homework becomes a family hassle, and we'll investigate how to prevent it from happening. To do so, we'll examine a number of real-life situations to see what works and what doesn't and why.

Does the following scene sound like one that frequently occurs at your house? It is seven o'clock. The television is blaring and a nine-year-old named Billy is transfixed in front of the screen. Turning off the TV, his mother sends him in to do his homework.

Only ten minutes pass before he is back, ready to take a "study break." His mother informs him that he hasn't studied long enough to take a break and sends him back to his room. A short while later Billy is once again back in the family room. He shrugs. "I can't figure my homework out. It just doesn't make any sense. I'll have to get help tomorrow."

If you were Billy's parent, what would you do? Try to help him with the work? Figure it's up to the teacher to give better directions and do nothing? Send him back to his room to try again? Tell him to forget it for tonight, but that you want him to check with his teacher first thing tomorrow?

Sometimes as a parent it seems handling your children and their homework is an impossible assignment in itself, but there are some guidelines that can help you. In Billy's case, what to do would depend a lot on past information, including whether he's done this sort of thing frequently before and how you feel about helping with homework.

Fortunately, Billy's situation was easily resolved by his perceptive mother. She asked him to show her what he didn't understand. "Can't I show you later?" he begged.

"No," replied his mother, "it's got to be right now."

Billy sighed. "Heck, I'll lose all track of what was going on in that movie. I sure hope Aaron's mom isn't making him do his homework or I'll never know what happened."

Billy's mom resolved from that point on that there was going to be an hour a day in which no television would be allowed. She said, "My kids had just rather drifted from being very interested in one program to being all involved in another. I told them that if they didn't have any homework, they could read a book of their choice for the no-TV hour. At first they complained, but they couldn't say much after they saw their grades improve."

BUT MOM, *I* DON'T HAVE ANY HOMEWORK

As a concerned parent, Mrs. Milner often asked her daughter Lisa if she had any homework. Lisa always replied no, that school was easy and that she had extra time in class to do any assignments, so

Mrs. Milner assumed everything was fine. She went to her daughter's first-term report card conference ready to hear an excellent report. Unfortunately, the teacher began by showing her Lisa's poor grades and then attributed them to lack of homework effort.

"Homework," interrupted Mrs. Milner, "but Lisa said that she never had any homework . . ."

There was silence in the room for a minute, and then Lisa's teacher said, "Would you like for me to tell you the kinds of things you should be expecting to see Lisa bring home as homework?"

Mrs. Milner listened carefully, and though she left school feeling quite upset, she had a course of action. She went home, papers in hand, to have a heart-to-heart talk with Lisa. Amid great tears, Lisa admitted to her mother that she'd been trying to do all her homework on the playground fifteen minutes before school started. "I just wanted to play after school, and I didn't want to bring home any books," she sobbed. "Besides, I was getting everything turned in."

Mrs. Milner insisted that they look at some of Lisa's returned papers together, and at first, Lisa was quite belligerent. She didn't ever want to see those papers again, but Mrs. Milner gently and firmly insisted that the two of them review some papers together. "Lisa," she pointed out, "the answer to this question confuses me. Can you read it?"

Lisa strained and pursed her lips. "I think I must have left some words out," she said, "but I know what I meant to say."

"I'll bet you do," said her mother, "because you're a smart girl, but how could your teacher know if you didn't take the time to show her?"

Lisa grinned sheepishly and admitted, "I guess she couldn't."

In analyzing how Mrs. Milner handled her daughter's nonperformance on homework, I'd give her an A+. For though she was very upset after leaving the report card conference, she made the best of the situation. She worked with the teacher, letting the teacher know that she wanted help in changing Lisa's homework patterns. The teacher in turn gave her hints as to approaching Lisa in a positive manner, and as a team, parent and teacher agreed to stay in touch at regular and frequent intervals about Lisa's homework habits. Mrs. Milner found out from the teacher exactly what kinds of homework she generally gave and approximately how much time a night the teacher estimated that they would take.

Mrs. Milner helped Lisa to see for herself how her poor homework habits were creating bad grades. While she didn't raise her voice or scream at Lisa, neither did she let the child wiggle out of accepting responsibility for what she had done. Also, she set up some concrete plans with Lisa and Lisa's teacher to help ensure better homework habits. Mrs. Milner resolved to begin asking Lisa to see some of her homework when it was completed, and to see some of it after it had been returned from the teacher.

After the conference with her teacher and her mother, Lisa too realized some valuable lessons. She found out that it wasn't enough just to get something down on paper, that she had to give herself sufficient time to get the homework not only done, but done to the best of her ability.

The same basic situation took a different turn at Melanie's house. When the teacher brought out Melanie's poorly done homework, Mrs. Torrance felt humiliated by her daughter's deceitfulness. She saw no need to make her embarrassment worse by telling the teacher that Melanie had said she didn't have any homework, so she said nothing. This left Melanie's teacher in the dark as to whether the child was doing her homework at the last minute or struggling over it at home and still producing such poor results.

By the time she arrived home, Mrs. Torrance was really furious. She walked in the house, turned off the television, and told her daughter she was grounded for the next month. "Look at these. Can you imagine how I felt with your teacher sitting there telling me she was quite concerned about your homework, and me not even knowing you had any homework?"

Melanie said nothing and Mrs. Torrance became even angrier. "I was absolutely humiliated, and now you can just forget about getting any help from me."

Kids who tell their parents they have no homework when in reality they do is nothing new. Teachers and parents run into the problems it creates every year, and while it is certainly easy to sympathize with Mrs. Torrance's anger at her daughter, there can be no doubt that the way Mrs. Milner handled the situation was better. As a high school teacher, I overhear many comments from teens who've learned over the years they've been in school to manipulate their parents into getting angry enough to avoid the real issue and leave the kids alone.

Of course, you certainly don't have to wait until there are problems with your children's homework to become involved. In fact, I'd recommend that you be a part of the homework process from the first time your child begins receiving at-home assignments. Establishing certain procedures from the onset can keep you from having to handle a lot of homework hassles later on with your children. It's easy to be a part of several steps in the homework process. The first step is for you to have a fairly specific idea of what is expected of your child. Begin by finding out if your particular school has a homework policy. Reading it will give you an idea of what the school feels your child should be doing at home. However, even within these guidelines, there are bound to be differences depending on the particular teacher, which is one reason why it is so important for you to attend your child's open house at the beginning of the year. At that time, the teacher will go over the homework policies in her classroom, and you will know from the start how much and what kinds of homework the teacher is assigning. Of course, that doesn't mean your child can't be successful and be spending more or less time on his homework. After all, teachers are only talking about the average. However, it does mean that you may want to check closely if the teacher has said she gives twenty minutes of homework a night, and your child has never brought home a book.

Next, it is absolutely crucial that you help your son or daughter develop the good study skills we discussed in the last chapter. In fact, helping your child learn organized study skills is the single most valuable thing you can do in ensuring him success with his homework. It will provide the maximum productivity in the minimum amount of time.

For example, I remember the case of Marvin. Marvin, his mother, and I were having a conference because they felt that Marvin was spending almost three times as long on his English homework as he had at the year's beginning, and something had to be wrong. His mother explained that he had his own desk in his bedroom, all the resource materials at it, and that he was well organized. Certain that I wasn't assigning any more homework than I had in the fall, I suggested that he keep a time sheet so we could see what was happening. "Write down what time you start studying, what you are studying, and each time you take a break, write that down as well."

Marvin's mother called me a week later to tell me the time sheet had provided the solution to Marvin's increased homework. He'd gotten his own telephone as a birthday present, and though he answered each call explaining that he had to finish his homework before he could talk, his concentration was being broken frequently. After each call it took him at least five minutes to get back into his studies, and then the phone would ring again, breaking his learning concentration.

That's just one example of why it's well worth remembering that ensuring that your child has good study skills doesn't mean just initially helping him establish them; it means checking up to make sure that they're all still firmly in place.

WHAT DOES YOUR CHILD DO IN SCHOOL?

Recently, I returned from a speaking engagement in which I addressed a large number of elementary school teachers. At the end of my speech, I asked them to write down the one best tip they would give parents toward helping their children be successful in school. The single most-repeated answer returned was this: *Tell parents to go over their children's work.* Show the kids that school is important by taking the few minutes each day to read through their papers. One third-grade teacher added, "I send home papers almost every day with instructions for kids to share their work with their parents. At the beginning of the year, I tell all the parents that each child will have a special home folder in which to carry returned papers, and that parents should be sure to check their children's home folders each day, and go over the papers in it. It just breaks my heart to look at some of the kids' folders. The work in them is never touched. When the folders finally get so full that nothing else can fit, I take the papers out."

Looking over your child's returned papers is so important. Even the mere act of his seeing you take them out and glance through them lends a feeling of significance to his work. Some parents feel that this task will take a tremendous amount of time that they just don't have, but it doesn't have to take more than a few minutes. You don't have to even thoroughly read each paper; just skim a few of them, and make some comment so that your child will know you've seen them.

Of course, if you wish to review the papers with your child, that's fine, but you should be careful not to be overly negative. It is really easy for even the best parent in the world to look at a math paper, and instead of saying, "How great that you got these twelve right," immediately zero in on "Why did you miss these two?" Does that mean that you can never comment on the areas that need improvement in your children's work? Of course not. Just make certain that your comments aren't geared only toward those things. For example, suppose Bobby brings home three papers. Two of them are so sloppily written that you are appalled at the penmanship; however, the third paper looks as if Bobby really prepared it with great care. You might try approaching Bobby with something like this. "Gee, Bobby, I like the way your penmanship looks on this paper. When you write neatly like this, you make sure that your teacher can read what you've said. Aren't you proud of this paper?"

Reviewing your child's graded homework not only tells the child that it has importance, but it also gives you a framework of what is being taught and what is being expected. It can also help you diagnose things that prevent later problems from occurring.

That's what Mrs. Jordan found out when she began cleaning out a drawer in the kitchen. "I'd stuck my son Donny's papers in there all year, and as I started sifting through them, I noticed that Donny consistently misspelled certain words." Mrs. Jordan went to her son's teacher and showed her.

"You know," replied that teacher, "you're absolutely right. He seems unclear about these three spelling rules. I'll work on them with him." In no time, Donny's spelling problem was corrected.

Now you may say, "Well, why didn't the teacher catch that in the first place?" and maybe the teacher should have caught the problem, but with hundreds of papers to grade each day, it is easy to miss a subtle pattern. Because your focus is only on your own child, you may be able to pinpoint things much more specifically than the teacher. Besides, whether or not the teacher should or shouldn't have caught Donny's spelling problem is really not the bottom line. The bottom line is that you want the best education you can get for your child, and if you can help ensure that by reviewing his homework, why not do so?

I've heard parents speak in front of their children, laughing and admitting how much they always hated getting homework, and that they really wished their kids didn't have any. Unfortunately, what follows is usually a very sketchy or missing number of homework assignments from the child. I, as his teacher, can never begin to mean to your child what you as his parent mean to him. If he feels that you think homework is a waste and you boast to your friends about how you beat the system in school, he will try to accomplish the same thing. If he knows that you are interested and invested in his homework, then chances are much greater that he will be interested as well. This became clear to me the first year I taught. One of my sophomore English students had been turning in each assignment in a thorough and neat manner. One day, I had given my students time to complete their grammar homework in class, and as I walked down the row, I saw the boy recopying his paper. "Oh, that's okay," I told him, "this is good enough the way it is."

"Maybe for you," he said, "but my mom looks over every assignment, and if it isn't done well, she tells me I've cheated myself."

THE RIGHT WAY TO HELP YOUR CHILD WITH HOMEWORK

So let's assume that you're taking an interest in your child's schoolwork, that you're looking through his papers, and that you've helped him develop good study skills. Is that it for helping with homework? Actually, that's just the beginning. For sooner or later, every child carries a book in to his parent, thrusts it into his mother's or father's hands, and says, "Can you help me? I don't understand."

It seems a simple enough request, but not only can it easily begin a family feud, the request can also end up estranging the parent-teacher partnership that should be working. Let's look at several situations to see why. Ralph is a boy in a top sixth-grade math group. He's stuck on his homework and takes the book into the kitchen to ask his mom for some help. She receives the math book with some hesitation. After all, it's been a lot of years since she's been in school, but after looking at them, she decides these problems really aren't hard; surely she can easily help her son. She begins to explain the process, but seems to be getting nowhere. She knows that their dinner is going to be overcooked if she can't get this cleared up soon. Furthermore, she's getting aggravated with Ralph because her explanation has been perfectly clear, and though her son is a bright boy, he says he still doesn't understand. "You're just not paying attention," she finally says.

"Yes, I am," says Ralph, looking defeated. "I just don't understand the way you're explaining it."

His mother is getting more frustrated by the minute as she begins again, and her voice rises a notch. Finally, she says, "Let me just go ahead and do one of these for you. Then maybe you'll see." She writes down the problem, and talks aloud as she works. "Subtract here, borrow from this column. See, that's how it's done. Do you understand?"

"Well," says Ralph, still confused and sensing his mother's ire, "maybe you could just help me a little with the rest. If you start these problems, I could finish them."

An hour later and with more than a couple of shouting matches, Ralph's homework is finished. Unfortunately, Ralph has not done most of it. Figuring that they could be at this all night, his mother has done the majority of the work. By the time she puts dinner on the table, she has lost her appetite, which is just as well because dinner has gotten too dried out to eat. Ralph too has a stomachache from the tension and, worst of all, he still doesn't really understand his math.

This situation is sad because Ralph's mother is a caring, concerned parent who really wanted to do her best to help her son with his homework, but she failed miserably. What could she have done to change things? There are some tips that would have worked not only for her, but you as well, when your child starts calling for homework help.

First of all, promise yourself that though you are happy to try to provide your child with some help, you are not going to do the work for him. If he truly cannot understand the assignments, his teacher needs to know about it. One of the primary reasons that teachers give homework is to check children's comprehension of a concept taught in class, and the child who returns with a perfect paper is telling the teacher to go ahead to the next concept. So though your child may beg you that he just has to get the assignment completed, you cannot do the work for him. In addition to giving the teacher false information, it reinforces your child's belief that he cannot possibly get the work done on his own. While it's true that your child may feel upset or concerned about not returning to school with the answers, if he is truly confused, you do him absolutely no favor by doing the work for him.

When your child first brings you his homework, see what it is that he seems to need help doing. If it looks as if his questions may take some time, evaluate whether you have the time to give him at that moment, and if not, ask him to work on something else, telling him at what time you can help him with this material. Part of the reason that Ralph's mother's frustration level rose so quickly was that she knew she should be in the kitchen finishing dinner. When she realized how confused Ralph was, she'd have been much better off to tell him to take a break and help him after dinner.

Kathy Bankoff, a Denver, Colorado, family counselor, says that sometimes homework can be used as a manipulative tool. "A child wants his parents' attention. He knows that one way to get it immediately is to bring in homework and say he needs help."

Bankoff recommends that in a very busy household with two working parents, it may be a wise idea to set aside a specific time every day that the child can get help with homework. If he needs no help, the parent will still spend that time with him, talking or playing a game. Says Bankoff, "By setting aside this special time, your child feels reassured that if he does need assistance with studies, you will always be there to give it to him, and if he has only been using help with homework as a means of guaranteeing your attention, he'll realize that it's no longer necessary to do so."

When you do begin helping your child with his homework, the best place to start is with the lesson directions. Ask your child to reread the directions for you. Tell him that you want to make certain that you both know what the lesson requires. Many kids balk at this. "I already know what I'm supposed to do," they say exasperatedly, "just help me with this problem."

Yet, almost daily, we teachers see students who have missed material simply beause they have failed to read all the directions. At the beginning of the year, I frequently give a quiz to try to point out to my students the importance of reading instructions. The quiz has twenty questions on it, and I tell the students they'll have to work rapidly to complete it in the next ten minutes. "Be sure to read the directions," I say before passing out the quiz. At the top are rather lengthy directions that end like this: "Do not answer any question on this quiz until you have read all twenty questions." The last question on the test then says, "This quiz has been given to see how well you pay attention to directions. You do not have to answer any of the above questions. Just write, 'I will carefully follow directions' on the bottom of your paper. Then watch all the kids work who didn't do so."

Of course, I don't end up counting the quiz for a grade, which is a good thing, because some years as many as 80 percent of the students fail to follow the directions. After having worked the whole quiz, they find the last question, and I hope it teaches a lesson they remember for the rest of the year: The work will always be ten times as difficult if they don't follow the directions about how to do it.

This problem of lazy direction reading doesn't apply only to high school students. My elementary school child came to me the other night for help with her math homework. "This problem can't be done," she said.

It didn't look as difficult to me as most of the others on the page. "Why not?" I asked.

"Because," she said with great certainty, "this chapter is on subtraction, so I know that these are all subtraction problems, but I think you have to add in the last two story problems. I don't understand."

I asked her to read the directions to me, and when she did so, she answered her own question, for right in the directions it clearly said that the last two problems were review questions from the last chapter.

Assuming that you have set aside a time to help with homework, and you've reread the directions with your child, keep in mind that it is important to guide him in what he should do, and not to do it for him. In a math or science problem, try to help him step by step in what he should do, even to the point of actually writing down each step as he figures it out. In a reading or social studies assignment, have him read the difficult passage aloud and then put it in his own words for you. After he's finished one problem or passage, have him do the next while you sit and watch. Perhaps one of the most difficult things to do is to not directly answer your child's questions. For example, if in a math problem, he says, "Do I multiply or divide here?" the easy answer would be to say, "Divide." However, that isn't going to help him a bit in the long run because he still hasn't figured out the process for himself. Granted, it is more time consuming, but you will be giving your child far more effective help if you say instead, "Well, why don't you try whichever you think is right, and we'll see what happens."

The process of self-discovery is difficult, but that knowledge is long-lasting, and helping a child to achieve self-discovery is the best kind of help you can give him. However, sometimes, in spite of having set aside your time, of having guided but not given answers, or developing a step-by-step plan of attack, your child is still totally confused. What then?

Parents are often tempted to feel upset, to think their child has put in enough time, and just complete the homework. As discussed above, this should never be done. However, it is important to let the teacher know that the assignment is incomplete because of lack of understanding and not just because of lack of effort. If the child is a young child, you may want to write a note to his teacher verifying the amount of time he spent on his homework, and attach it to his paper. Teachers appreciate knowing that the child was confused and not just too lazy to do the work assigned. If the child is an older child, he should write his own note on his paper saying that he tried to do the assignment, and describe at what point he became confused. It is important for an older child to begin to take responsibility for himself and establish his own communication with his teacher.

If you feel very bad about sending him to school with unfinished papers, remember that your ultimate goal in helping him with his homework is to help him acquire the skills he needs for success, and simply doing the work for him can never accomplish that.

There are, however, several things you can do to remove potential roadblocks. For example, you might consider whether your child is experiencing a situation like that of Roy. Roy was one of the most talented, charming, intelligent students I'd ever had in my class. He was the kind of child that every parent wished he could point to as his own. Even his parents shook their heads at all that Roy was able to accomplish. Not only was he taking all accelerated classes, but he was also on the baseball team, had the lead in the school musical, participated three nights a week at his church's bible-study group, and was an officer in the church youth group.

One day while taking a simple quiz in class, Roy suddenly ripped up his paper, threw it in the wastebasket, and stormed out of the room. The class sat in stunned silence; no one could quite believe what had happened, and no one had any idea what had caused it.

It took some extensive discussion among Roy, his counselor, and his parents before even Roy fully understood what had happened. One by one he'd taken on an additional responsibility. By themselves, none of the increased honors or activities had seemed that extensive. His parents were aware of the fact that he was trying to do a great deal, but he seemed to be successfully getting it all done. Neither he nor they realized the increased pressure until he just snapped. During the counseling session he admitted that in order to keep up his grades, in addition to all the other activities, he was going to bed at midnight, then getting up at four in the morning to do homework. He'd finally broken under the stress.

Though this case seems extreme, it is representative of a major cause of unsuccessful homework. The child simply has too many other things scheduled to have time left to schedule homework. One nine-year-old girl reeled off her week; each day after school came a different activity: a piano lesson, daily practice, Girl Scouts, ballet, etc. By the time she'd finished a day of school and her afternoon activity she was exhausted.

At one point when I taught seniors, 80 percent of my students worked after school, and many of them worked until ten in the evening or even later. Their main reason for wanting to work was to be able to afford gas and insurance on a car. Getting them to do any homework was a constant hassle. "Mrs. Fields," said one boy, "how can you possibly give me a paper to write. Don't you know that I have a job?"

I have no quarrel with the child who really needs to work to help sustain the family, but if your son or daughter is only working long hours to buy more clothes or to have more spending money, please consider what you are allowing him to do to his education. The students in my class in the $60 jeans and $100 sweaters who fall asleep at their desks break my heart. HELP YOUR CHILD SUC-CESSFULLY COMPLETE HIS HOMEWORK BY MAKING CERTAIN THAT HE HAS TIME TO GET IT DONE. If that means having to tell him that he can't work until midnight or that he must choose between two after-school activities, then do so. Leave him time to relax and time to do homework. In the long run you'll be doing him a large favor.

_____

   Another valuable way that you can help your child be successful with school is to extend the reach of his homework into his everyday life. Kids sometimes see school as an artificial environment having little relationship to their lives after the final dismissal bell. However, almost any teacher can attest to the interest and improvement in a child's work when the parent has shown that work is valuable at home. For example, one fourth-grade girl's mother noticed that her child was getting homework on multiplication. "This is so dumb," complained the child to her mother.

   The mother said nothing, but the next night, she got out her recipe book. "I'd really like to make this casserole, but it's only for four, and I'm supposed to bring enough for twelve to your brother's football potluck. Do you think you could help me figure out the amounts of the ingredients?"

   The child was intrigued, and furthermore, was able to see concrete results from what she was learning. If the ingredients were incorrectly multiplied, she would know it as soon as she tasted the casserole. Suddenly, the girl's homework seemed more important to her. Though her teacher had mentioned that the children would need to use math in all aspects of life, this little girl didn't pay much attention. However, when using correct multiplication meant that the child was going to make or ruin a casserole, knowing that her mother planned to serve it, the idea of learning how to multiply became much more important.

   Even an idle comment can help reinforce your child's homework. A father who noticed his son working on a math unit on decimals said, "I'm sure glad they're teaching you that math. Pay attention to it. I've seen guys lose a contract because their calculator won't work, and they can't do their own figures."

   The boy's eyes grew large. "Why don't those guys just go back to their office and figure it out on another calculator?"

"Son," replied his father, "you don't understand. Lots of the time, you make or break a deal on the spot."

WHAT KIND OF HOMEWORK IS YOUR CHILD GETTING?

Teachers give homework for many reasons; however, since it usually means more work for the teacher as well, I don't know of any teachers who give it just "to give kids something to do," although I've heard many students offer that as the reason. What are the real reasons for homework? Knowing what the teacher's intent is behind the work may make it seem more reasonable to you.

Homework is a way to give a student the opportunity to enrich and further explore an idea initially presented in class. A high school history teacher may go over the Bill of Rights in class, and then to give it further meaning may ask each student to find something in the news that applies to one of the Bill of Rights.

Homework allows a child a chance to practice a new skill learned. The child who has just been taught how to make a cursive E knows what is involved, but the teacher may want him to practice at home so that he feels comfortable with the motion.

Homework that asks students to study for a test requires the students to review material that has been covered in the past and make certain that they remember it. However, homework assignments do much more than cover a particular topic. In many instances, they develop traits and skills that will allow the child to be successful in school and in life, and that is why it is important for a parent to help develop a good attitude toward homework in his child. It allows the child the opportunity to develop further reading skills, better thought organization, and develops the ability to organize materials, read carefully, learn to follow written directions, and think creatively.

Of course, there are two types of homework given: the work initially assigned as homework, and the work some students bring home because although it was intended as classwork, they weren't able to finish it in class. It's important for a parent to know the

difference between the two, but how can you know which type
of work your child is bringing home? Sometimes a teacher will
clearly indicate that the work coming home is incompleted class
work. However, many teachers do not do this, so from time to time,
it doesn't hurt to ask your child if everyone in the class has this
assignment. Usually, after some hesitating, he'll admit that only the
kids who didn't finish have this work as homework. If this situation
is happening to your child only once in a while, there is no reason
for concern; however, if your child begins bringing home unfinished
work on a fairly regular basis, it is time to make some inquiries.
The best place to begin is with your own child, asking him if he can
figure out any reasons he often has unfinished work. More than
likely, he'll begin by saying, "I don't know." A natural parental
response is to offer a possible reason for the problem; however, it's
probably better to let the child take responsibility for his own actions and let him supply a reason. If he cannot seem to arrive at any
answers, the parent should suggest a conference with the child and
the teacher.

One of two things will usually result from the conference. Either
the child is having academic problems with the class and the extra
homework may signal a need for help, or the child is having problems taking responsibility for his work, and his homework problems
signal a need for better study and organization skills. *Neither thing
means your child is a failure.* However, by recognizing these homework problems and identifying the cause of them, you can help your
child solve them. If you find yourself facing either of these dilem-
mas, pay particular attention to the chapters in this book on dealing
with academic problems and on developing study skills.

IF YOU DON'T AGREE WITH YOUR CHILD'S HOMEWORK

If your child begins bringing home work for which you can see
absolutely no purpose, by all means, contact the teacher. You probably cannot help your child see the importance of doing it if you
cannot understand the importance yourself. However, be sure to

remember the rules for good conferencing discussed in Chapter One. I suggest that you begin your homework conference by summarizing what you think the child has been asked to do. Sometimes, it is not at all what the teacher actually assigned and sometimes, there is a definite reason for it having been given. For example, Tim's mother was quite concerned when she saw her son writing twenty spelling words a hundred times each. "Why are you doing that?" she asked Tim.

He shrugged. "I guess my teacher just needed to give us some busy work."

Tim's mother was upset. She saw no reason for the assignment, and obviously, neither did Tim. At first, she thought she'd let it go, but the longer she saw Tim working on the pages of words, the more determined she became to contact the teacher. When she finally did so, she said that she'd noticed Tim working on writing the same spelling word over and over again and wondered if this was the way spelling was usually handled.

The teacher laughed. "Only as an absolute last resort. We've gone over the words in class. We've broken them apart and discussed them, we've written sentences using the words. We've taken quizzes on the words, and I've offered a couple of review sessions on them, but if a student didn't come to the review and still kept missing words I gave this assignment to him. Evidently, in Tim's case it worked because he finally got a hundred percent on a spelling test, but he certainly could have done it far less painfully if he'd paid attention from the beginning."

Another time that you may wish to check with the teacher is if you feel uncertain about how much help you are allowed to give your child. Consider what you would do if you were this eight-year-old child's mother. He said, "We're supposed to write a story. I have a really long one in my head, but my hand hurts to write it and recopy it."

The mother and teacher had discussed the child's motor-development problems previously, and the mother put in another call to the teacher. "I'd really like to encourage Adam's creativity. Would it be all right if I just typed his story as he dictated it to me?"

"I'd prefer not," explained the teacher. "If you do that, I'll have no way of knowing how Adam spells, or whether he's using the end punctuation we just learned."

The two of them talked further and finally arrived at a compromise. If Adam would write one draft of his story and put any corrections he wanted on the paper, his mother would retype the story. However, she promised to type it just as Adam had written it. To everyone's amazement, once Adam knew he was freed of the laborious physical rewriting of his story, he wrote a six-page fantasy.

The situation did not end nearly as well for a high school student named Greg. His father recalls, "My son asked me to have my secretary type a report he'd been working very hard on because he wanted the report to look neater. I agreed. My secretary told me that there were quite a few grammatical and spelling errors in the report. Now, I knew he'd worked real hard on the report, and I figured he's only a kid, so I told her to fix any mistakes she saw. Then my son got a bad grade for not doing his own work. I only thought I was helping."

Sighed the teacher, "For three weeks, we worked on punctuation in my class. This paper was done in part to show me whether the kids could apply the rules we learned to their writing. Now all I know is that Mr. Allingham's secretary knows the rules. How can parents be so . . ." she groped for the right word and shook her head.

If you're in doubt, a short note or a brief call to the teacher may give you some effective guidance on the amount of help you may offer. In general, however, you might keep this in mind. Most teachers are happy to have parents look over their children's finished work and make suggestions about it. However, there is a big difference between noting that there are several spelling errors in a paper or even circling the misspelled words and telling the child to check them in the dictionary, and simply going through and correcting all the spelling yourself. It's fine to glance through a set of math problems and suggest that there might be a couple of errors; however, if ten out of twelve problems are wrong, you shouldn't be the one to rework them.

Your reaction to your child's homework can play a big part in how successful he is in completing it. Recently, an elementary school announced a patriotic-float contest for its students to enter. Three first graders arrived at their respective homes, all excitedly telling their parents how much they wanted to enter and win. Each of the parents' initial reactions was almost the same, a feeling that this was quite a difficult project for such a young child. Thus, since it was not required homework, the first parent simply forbade his child to enter, saying that the whole thing was nonsense. The second parent decided that her child could enter a float but would need some help. She thought for a day or two and made several suggestions which he could pretty well do alone. In the final result, he produced his float by putting a board on an old wagon, and arranging his small toys on the board each holding a flag or waving a patriotic saying. The third parent felt that having her child win would be a very positive experience for him since, if he started getting the feel of winning in the first grade, it would carry through the rest of his schooling. She figured that every parent would be helping tremendously and, thankful that she was fairly artistic, she created a beautiful sculpture. The child got to do a few of the finishing details.

All three of these people were concerned parents who were taking a real interest in their child's education. Each parent genuinely thought he or she was handling this voluntary homework assignment well, but the children themselves were not so easily fooled. The third child did win a place for his float, but he told bystanders only that the ribbon was going to make his mother very happy. Even though he was just six years old, he knew exactly whose project it had been. The first child watched longingly as his friends marched in the parade, wishing he'd gotten to be part of the fun. Only the second child came away feeling a sense of success and a willingness to go forward again in trying the next unusual challenge.

A Homework Survey

- *Are you aware of each of your child's teachers' homework requirements and philosophies?* It is ever so much easier to help your child if you understand what is being expected of him. When he comes to you and says, "I don't understand why I got a B on this report. Look at all the pretty pictures I drew," you can reply that last year's history teacher thought pictures added a lot to reports, but this year's teacher thinks students are more grown up and wants them to concentrate more on explanations of what actually happened.

● *Has your child been doing his homework on a regular basis in the past?* Think about whether your child knows that there is a definite time in which the television must remain off and homework must begin. If the attitude toward homework around your house has been fairly relaxed in the past, and your child has begun having trouble, it's possible that your child may lack the organizational skills and the discipline to get his work done. You can't expect him to have just suddenly acquired organization and discipline because the workload has increased. Assist your child in setting forth guidelines and limitations, in developing a study spot and time.

If your child has been doing his homework regularly but has suddenly stopped, it may be a good indication that there are other problems at school, and it would be an excellent idea to contact the teacher.

● *Have you examined the graded papers that have been returned to your child?* Do you go through your child's papers on a regular basis? If you haven't been doing so, you really need to begin. Approach reviewing your child's work positively, and let your child know that you're excited about seeing more of his assignments.

Many parents who were quite diligent about doing this when their children were small bow to their teenagers' cry for independence, and in doing so, they pay little attention to their kids' work. Yet a recent study by the National Center for Education Statistics of 58,000 students showed that 88 percent of A students indicated a high degree of parental supervision.

● *Does your child seem to be having trouble in all his major academic areas or in just one area?* Problems in every academic area may suggest that there is need for special testing. Perhaps your child has a learning disability that has not been identified.

Consider whether these difficulties have been ongoing or whether they have just begun. Sudden drops in academic understanding in every subject may suggest problems that are not just academic. The child may be preoccupied with a social problem; he may be concerned about a situation at home, or he may be involved in substance abuse. I've spoken with upset parents who've waited too long to get involved. They all repeated virtually the same thing. "My child never had problems before. I just thought it would go away." It is best not to ignore the situation, but to try to investigate it immediately.

- *How have you responded to your child's past pleas for your help in getting homework done?* As mentioned earlier in this chapter, if your child feels that asking you to help him with his homework is a sure way to get your undivided attention, you are likely to get asked a lot. Make sure that you have time set aside for your child so that homework is not his "in" to getting to you.

  Also, every child gets stuck for a homework answer. If you respond to his plea for help by giving outright answers to the questions, he'll soon figure out that the minute he becomes confused, it's a lot easier to ask you than it is to even attempt to figure out the item on his own.

- *How has your child responded in the past to your efforts at helping him do his homework?* Even many full-time teachers report that the hardest student to help with homework is their own child. If every time you try to help your child with homework, your house turns into a battle zone, it may be better for you to avoid doing so. Let the teacher explain it the next day. From her he may accept that the paper's topic sentence isn't clear, while he may burst into tears at the same words from you.

  You may want to refer your child to a friend, a professional tutor, a school homework hotline, or to investigate peer tutoring as alternatives to your helping if you feel that your help is counterproductive. However, remember that doesn't mean you shouldn't still look over your child's completed work. Regardless of whether you are the one to help him or have someone else help him, you should still stay on top of what is happening with the homework.

- *How do you feel about helping with homework?* Some parents feel very uncomfortable being thrust into this role. "I was a terrible student," confided one mother. "Whenever I try to help my daughter, I'm afraid it only points out how inadequate I was in school, and I don't want her to think I'm stupid. She'll lose respect for me."

  "I know I should be more patient," admits another mother, "but I just can't stand it. It takes my son so long to figure out such simple problems. I try not to get short-tempered, but my son knows I'm getting frustrated. I can feel my skin start to crawl every time he brings me his math book."

  For whatever reason, if you really hate the idea of helping your child with his homework, it is better not to do so than to make the homework atmosphere completely unpleasant. Investigate the resources mentioned above, such as homework hotlines, peer tutors, professional tutors, or staying after school for extra teacher help. You can still be a homework consultant to your child and let him know that homework is important by looking over his completed papers and providing him with a good study atmosphere. Don't let yourself be consumed with guilt if you just cannot handle working with your child. If you communicate to him that schooling is important and that you believe he can succeed and will aid him in getting additional help if he needs it, you can do much more good than fighting with him over every specific homework assignment.

THE FUTURE OF HOMEWORK

One thing seems certain: Homework is in for the eighties. According to a 1983 Gallup Opinion Poll, 61 percent of elementary school parents and 65 percent of high school parents feel that their children are not made to work hard enough in school and on homework. That kind of public support suggests that homework will not disappear; in fact, responding to public demand, schools may actually give their students more at-home assignments. Many of today's parents see homework as a no-cost way to continue the school day and expand the learning process. It is a way to enrich a program or give students more time for example and practice before going on to another concept. By the time recess, lunch, PE, or music and other nonacademic parts of the school day are totaled, children may only be spending a few hours a day learning academics in school, and parents are realizing that if the teacher is to accomplish all that she can, homework must become an important supplemental tool.

The research data is supporting parents' perceptions. "Homework's Powerful Effects on Learning" contains a synthesis of fifteen studies about homework, and concludes that there is much higher achievement by elementary and secondary students when homework is required, especially if the homework is graded or discussed. Walberg, a Research Professor of Education at the University of Chicago, and his associates conclude "there seems little doubt that homework has substantial effects on students' learning. There is even less doubt that American students, on the average, allocate comparatively little time to it—perhaps about one sixth of the amount of time they spend watching television, which may be useless if not harmful."*

---

* Herbert J. Walberg, Rossane A. Paschal, and Thomas Weinstein, "Homework's Powerful Effects on Learning," *Educational Leadership,* April 1985, pp. 76–79.

SIX

TIPS
TO IMPROVE
YOUR CHILD'S
TEST SCORES

T errifying because
E verything
S hows
T hat I don't know.

This student-written poem got a sympathetic chuckle from the other students in the class, and all the kids agreed that it wasn't much fun to take tests. However, there's no doubt that some kids have a big edge over others at exam time, and it isn't just because they are the smarter students. It's because they've learned the tips and strategies for successful test-taking. Yet far too many kids go through school without ever being aware of what these special strategies are. Why shouldn't your child be one of the children who has that special edge in taking exams? This chapter will give you test-taking strategies to share with your children, as well as explain how to deal with test anxieties and what all the terminology of standard testing means.

Your child is certainly quite normal if he feels a little nervous before beginning a test. In fact, it may be a good sign. His concern over the test has helped motivate him to study the material, and it will help him to put forth his best effort on each question. However, for some children, test anxiety goes far beyond feeling a little nervous. It can make a child so frightened that he is actually unable to display his knowledge. Here's how one fifteen-year-old girl named Cindy described her feelings. "My grades hadn't been so good, but I decided that I wanted to do better, so I really studied for the last test we took. It didn't help. I wanted to get a good grade so much that even before I walked into the classroom, I could start to feel my mouth get real dry, and my stomach start feeling kind of sick. I thought that maybe if I sat down at my desk and went over my notes before the bell rang, I'd be able to review one last time, but everything started looking blurry, and I started thinking that there was so much to remember. Then the boy behind me asked me a question, and I didn't know anything about it. That did it. I was sure I was going to fail. The teacher started passing out the tests, and by the time I got mine, I was so upset that I really could barely remember my name. I just sat there trying not to cry."

Probably everyone has had that kind of test experience once in his life, but it certainly isn't something you'd like your child to go through. There are some ways that you can help him avoid test anxiety. You know your own child, and while it's important to make him feel that schoolwork is significant and tests are worthwhile, be careful that you don't put such undue pressure on him about a test that he panics. Too much anxiety is definitely counterproductive.

If you know your child tends to get overly nervous about tests, offer to quiz him when he has finished studying for the test, and when you do quiz him, concentrate not just on what he gets wrong but emphasize how much he has learned and how many answers he has gotten correct. Help him see himself in a positive light. Frequently, the students I've dealt with who have tremendous test anxiety have a very low self-image or an absolute perfectionist nature. There is an old saying "Think you can or think you can't; either way, you're right!" That applies to test-taking well. The child who feels he can't do well on the test usually fulfills his own prophecy. So, while there is no substitute for learning the material to be tested, once you feel that your child has done this, there is a great deal to be gained by making him feel good about himself and the test he will take.

There are a few other tips you can share with him as well. Advise him not to take out his notes for one last quick review before the test. If he's already learned the material, he'll know it on the test. All the last-minute review can do is to shake his confidence and make him unsure that he really has learned everything. For the same reason, tell him to try to ignore pretest chatter between kids. As one fourth-grade teacher observed, a boy came into a class and turned to the girl next to him. "Quick," he said, "tell me how you multiply fractions again!"

The girl took out a pencil and paper and began to try to explain. "That can't be," said the boy. "I thought it was supposed to be done like this." By the time the test started, the girl had begun to doubt herself. Ironically, there was no problem on their test in which fractions had to be multiplied. However, the girl was so shaken when she got the test that she lost five minutes trying to calm herself down and make herself believe that she did know what she was doing.

If your child gets a drink of water, and uses the restroom before testing begins, he'll feel physically more comfortable. If he brings all of his supplies, he'll know that he has the materials to be successful on the test; and if he arrives at the test with time to spare, sits down taking some deep, relaxing breaths, and tells himself not to worry, that he'll do the best he possibly can do, he'll have a big edge in overcoming test anxiety.

TEST-TAKING TIPS

Although kids spend a great deal of their school lives taking tests and studying the material that will be on them, they spend little or no time at all learning how to take a test. That's truly unfortunate, for while good strategy in test-taking is no substitute for learning the material, it *can* be used to raise test scores and make school easier for your child. Best of all, once learned, children can use these techniques from grammar school right through college.

I've corrected over 20,000 tests and quizzes in my teaching career, and the experience has taught me a great deal. For one thing, while the teachers' purpose in giving a test is to evaluate student knowledge of material, there's no doubt that savvy test takers have a decided advantage in maximizing their scores.

Recent research from two studies found that "If an average student performs at the fiftieth percentile (on a standardized test), that same student would probably score at over the sixtieth percentile if exposed to test-wiseness training."* Test-wiseness can involve such simple things as knowing the mechanics of taking the test to developing a strategy for answers to questions which are confusing.

Jenni took a test that required her only to blacken in circles on an answer sheet. When everyone else got his test back, Jenni got none. Neither did the boy who sat three seats down from her. The teacher called them both to her desk and said, "I have two tests here with no names and no way to determine whose is whose. Perhaps neither of you should receive any credit for taking the test." While Jenni's teacher eventually relented, there is nothing that irritates a teacher more than receiving a test with no name. It adds one extra step to the teacher's grading process and may cost point loss for the student. Even if the teacher doesn't take off points, she begins reading the test feeling aggravated. Teaching your child to avoid this problem is certainly easy enough. Just get him in the habit of PUTTING HIS NAME ON EVERY TEST BEFORE HE EVER BEGINS THE FIRST QUESTION.

Let's see if you're ready for a little test yourself. I'm going to give you some examples of students who did poorly on tests. See if you can figure out why.

Bobby walked out of his English class fighting back tears. After he'd studied so hard for this test, he knew he'd done poorly. The teacher was an absolute witch; she'd made the test so long that it was impossible for him to finish. He'd had to leave the last four

---

* Berliner and Casanova, "Should Students Be Made Test-Wise?," *Instructor Magazine,* February 1986, p. 23.

questions blank even though he'd wasted no time in starting the first question immediately.

What was Bobby's mistake? A common one to be sure. Bobby hadn't taken time to read the directions thoroughly. If he had, he would have known that he was only to pick three questions to answer out of the seven on the first section of the test. However, in his haste to begin, Bobby hadn't read that information and by the time he'd finished answering all seven questions, he didn't have time to complete the entire test, and he didn't get a very good grade. Rule two then is always to READ THE DIRECTIONS BEFORE BEGINNING A TEST. If there are separate directions for each section of the test, do not assume that they are the same. Read each set of directions. Test directions can actually be construed as hints to help your child score well. Have him be on the lookout for words such as *fill in, circle, supply, choose the item that does not belong, answer yes or no, support answers with examples from the book, underline, match,* etc. This may seem like much ado over nothing, but it does make a big difference. One teacher found that she was able to improve her students' test scores just by making them stop and circle each verb in each set of directions before the children could take the test. Teach your child that the time he spends carefully reading the directions is time well spent in improving any test score.

Along with reading each set of directions, your child should quickly PREVIEW THE TEST to get an idea of the types and number of questions being asked. Teachers frequently put a heavily weighted essay question at the end of the test. Imagine the horror of a child who has been methodically working through several pages of multiple-choice questions turning to the last page to discover it is worth the most points and he has left himself no time to finish it.

Here's another testing situation. Can you see how this student sabotaged himself? Alan was taking a history test about which he felt fairly confident. He usually did all right in history, and he'd studied for this test. He skimmed the questions quickly. They didn't seem too hard. Here is an example of one question. "Which of the following was not a part of the original thirteen colonies?"

a. Rhode Island
b. Connecticut
c. Pennsylvania
d. Arizona
e. Rhode Island, Connecticut, and Pennsylvania

"I know that," thought Alan, and marked "e." Even when he got the test back, he failed to see his error. He raised his hand and told the teacher she'd mismarked the test. Why?

Alan had read the question too quickly. He'd anticipated what he thought it should say instead of what it did say, and he'd failed to notice the word "not." His sloppy reading cost him the credit for a question to which he really did know the answer. It's good to skim quickly in previewing a test, but it's important when actually answering the questions to MAKE SURE YOU READ EVERY WORD IN THE QUESTION CAREFULLY.

Patty was the first one finished on the science test. With a huge sigh of relief, she turned in her paper and put her head on her desk to rest for the balance of the hour. It felt good to have the test behind her, and she was rather proud of having been the first one to finish. Unfortunately, her pride turned to despair when the graded tests were returned. Why? She'd made many careless errors that could have been corrected by simply taking the time to proofread her answers.

Teach your child that there is no reward for being the first one finished on a test. IF YOUR CHILD FINISHES A TEST EARLY, HE SHOULD SPEND ANY EXTRA TIME PROOFREADING HIS ANSWERS. It can give him an extra edge in making certain that he has followed directions, that he has answered every question, and that he has done his best work. This seems like an easy enough concept, but many children fight it. Perhaps because we are a society that stresses winning so much, children see some value in finishing first. Please remind your child that taking a test isn't a race to a finish line.

Another tip you might want to give your child is to ANSWER THE EASY QUESTIONS FIRST. There are several advantages to this.

First of all, it gives the child a feeling of confidence and helps reduce test anxiety. He thinks to himself, "Hey, this test isn't so bad. I know that answer, and that one, and that one."

From a scoring standpoint, answering the easy questions first makes sense because it is a fast way to maximize point totals. The child will have used a minimum of time to make certain he gets to all the "cinch" point questions. There's only one problem with this. MAKE CERTAIN THAT YOUR CHILD MARKS CLEARLY ANY QUESTIONS WHICH HE'S SKIPPED AND PLANS TO COME BACK TO LATER. It's easy to get so caught up in the test-taking that he forgets he's skipped a particular question, and thus, he never goes back to answer it.

Help your child develop enough savvy to know that HE SHOULDN'T JUST GIVE UP ON THE HARD QUESTIONS. He should try checking some of the key words in the question, rephrasing the question, or glancing through his test to see if another question is about the same subject and might provide a part of the answer to this question. Unless he will be less penalized for blanks than incorrect answers, IF ALL ELSE FAILS, HE SHOULD GUESS AT THE ANSWER.

Key your child in to the idea of learning to BUDGET HIS TIME ON A TEST. Sarah is a bright fifteen-year-old sophomore who stormed into my class the other day and announced to her friend that she'd just failed her geometry test. "There was this one proof. I knew I should be able to do it, but I just couldn't get it to work. I was so mad that I just kept trying, and then I ran out of time to finish the rest of the test." Sarah's plight is not so uncommon; however, it can be avoided if a child learns to be a clock watcher and not allow himself to spend too much time on any one item of a test.

Finally, make sure that your child gets in the habit of TAKING ENOUGH PENCILS, PENS, AND PAPER TO TESTS. Having the wrong materials creates instant test anxiety at just the time a student least wants it. Let me give you an example. On a literature test earlier this year, a boy walked into my class. "Mrs. Fields," he said, "I really studied for this test. I'm so nervous about it; I hope I do well." Minutes later, as I instructed everyone to clear his desk, I saw this boy frantically begin to search for a pen. By the time he finally borrowed one from another student, everyone else was waiting for him to clear his desk so they could get their tests. Midway through the exam, I saw him begin to bang the pen against his paper. I walked over to him, and he looked defeated. "This pen keeps skipping," he explained. "I need to borrow another one." His test paper looked a mess, and though I loaned him a working pen, he'd wasted much time, effort, and energy on the mechanics of being able to take the test instead of being able to direct all his concentration to its content.

TEST TYPES

Perhaps your test days in school are still quite vivid to you, but if they aren't, here's a quick review. When the teacher announces that it's test time, your child will either be given an essay exam or will take one of four basic types of objective tests: multiple choice, true-false, fill-in-the-blank, or matching. Each requires different strategies.

Multiple-Choice Tests

1. Teach your child to eliminate obviously incorrect answers. That means that instead of having a one-in-five chance of getting the question right, he may be able to immediately narrow it to a one-in-two chance.

2. Have him try reading the stem of the question with each answer. Often the best answer sounds the best to the ear. That's because it was designed by the teacher to make one complete statement.

3. Suggest that your child read the question and supply the answer himself before he reads the choices given. If he knows what answer he is trying to find, he will be much less likely to be trapped by a teacher's wrong-but-almost-sounds-right type of answer.

4. Go over the following words with your child: *usually, almost always, often, sometimes,* and *frequently.* These words quite often appear in correct answers. They are qualifier type words that make it easier for a statement to be true. By the same token, words like *never, none, always,* and *all* tend to be found in incorrect answers because few things in life are stated in absolutes. If your child understands this, he will have a big edge in taking tests.

5. Tell your child that if he's really stumped on a question, he should mark the spot and come back to it later. It is entirely possible that other questions on the test will give him clues as to the answer in the confusing one.

I saw a girl in my class use this strategy just last week. I'd written a test question that said, "This story was ironic in which of the following instances," and listed five different choices. The girl was unsure about the answer because she wasn't as clear as she might have been on the definition of irony. However, later in the test, I'd given a matching item about irony, and when she saw the actual definition in the matching choices, it refreshed her memory enough to go back and answer the specific example from the multiple-choice question earlier on the test.

Matching Tests

Many teachers like to give matching tests because they're less work to write than a multiple-choice test; they can easily cover a lot of material, and they're much easier to grade than essay tests. Knowing that he will run into these tests throughout his schooling, your child may want to pay special attention to these simple strategies in taking matching tests.

1. Remind your child to read the directions carefully. Most matching tests say that once you've used an answer, you may not reuse it. However, there are some teachers who give directions like this: "Some matching choices may be used several times. Some may not be used at all." You can imagine what happens to the child's test score if he fails to read the directions and just assumes that he can only use an answer once. His frustration level rises almost as rapidly as his grade on the test falls.

2. Assuming it is a type of matching test that allows the use of a choice only once, have your child learn to cross out a choice as soon as he's used it. That will leave fewer choices to deal with in making a decision on the next items.

3. Have your child skim the test quickly and then do the easy items first. Again, this is a good strategy to narrow the number of choices with which he must work when he gets to the harder questions.

4. Teach him that as he reads the question, he should answer it himself before looking at the answers provided on the test. That will help him focus on the right answer as he goes through a long list of possible choices.

Fill-in-the-Blank Tests

Some students think these tests are easier than multiple choice or matching because there are no wrong answers given and, thus, they can't be confused by them. Other students complain that these tests are much harder because they have to think of the right answer on their own, which can be more difficult than just having to recognize it. Either way, there are several tips to make it easier to take a fill-in-the-blank test.

1. Remind your child to read the question twice. Make sure that he understands exactly what is being asked for before he starts to fill in the blank.

2. Tell your child not to assume that the space he's been given for an answer has the correct number of blanks in it. Many teachers feel that this gives an unnecessary clue, and purposely don't indicate how many answers are needed to be correct.

For example, the other day I asked a question on the test that read "Name all the essays we read that dealt with children. _____ ." Though we'd read two essays on the subject, I found, much to my surprise, that several good students named only one. When I asked them why, they said, "You had only one blank."

Students need to concentrate on the questions, not the blanks.

Essay Tests

Though they are more difficult to grade, I like to give essay tests because it helps children learn to express their thoughts logically and concisely under pressure. It involves student creativity, clear thinking, and organization. How to be successful in taking them:

1. Students must read the question carefully. A single essay question is usually worth many points. It's time well spent, therefore, to spend a few extra minutes dissecting the question before attempting an answer. Teach your child to read the question twice, then ask himself what it is the question is asking. Though I always remind students to please read the questions carefully, on every test there is at least one student who later complains, "I knew the answer. I just misread the question!"

2. Help your child learn to get to the main idea immediately. An easy trick that makes points on essay questions is to turn the question around and begin the essay with it as the opening statement. For example, "Which animal was your favorite character in *Animal Farm* and why?" The best way to begin the answer might be to say, "My favorite character in the book *Animal Farm* was the _____ ." Changing the question into the topic sentence of his essay assures your child and his teacher that the answer is going to be on target instead of straying off onto something else.

3. Every student should create a brief outline of what he intends to say before he begins to write the answer to an essay question. This organized approach almost always assures extra points on an exam. The outline should include the major idea that is being stated, plus a list of each item that supports that main idea. Several details should be listed under each of those items of support. Then the student should look at his outline, evaluate his time, and decide which things he will use.

Though it may sound more complex to write an outline first, it is actually a time-saver. Help your child realize that writing that outline keeps him focused on the topic. It organizes and structures his thoughts, and it makes certain that he'll back thoughts with reasons or examples. As a teacher who has read countless essay test answers, I can usually tell which students have taken the extra few minutes to write an outline.

4. The conclusion is the final important part to an essay question. It need not be long, but it should sum up the important parts of the answer.

5. Finally, here's a tip that is guaranteed to help your child maximize his points on any essay test: He should always make certain his penmanship is neat and he has proofread his test before handing it in. Chances are that even if he isn't really sure what the answer should be, if he's attempted to write something about the subject, and he has used good spelling, grammar, and punctuation, he'll get many more points than the student who has simply thrown up his hands and given up because he's unsure of the answer.

WHEN THE TEACHER ANNOUNCES A TEST

The specific test-taking strategies we've examined will certainly help your child succeed on exams. However, your child can begin to improve his grades by knowing what to do from the minute a teacher announces that there will be a test. How? Have him follow these tips to make certain that he is properly prepared.

Teachers usually take the time to tell students what will be covered on a test. Tell your child to tune in to the review. That seems like simple enough advice, but if you could be an invisible person in the back of your child's classroom, I wonder if you'd see that he was the child who was using the test review time to finish another assignment, write a note to a friend, or wander off into a daydream. Kids often figure test review time doesn't count because nothing new is being presented, but this time is crucial to doing well with less study effort. Your child should be taking careful notes on every area the teacher says will be covered on the test. Not only will it be an obvious aid in helping your child decide what areas he needs to study, but in addition, it's a tremendous psychological boost for the child to know he won't encounter surprises on the test.

One of the best things you can teach your child is that if he is uncertain about material which might appear on a test, he should ask. Sometimes a teacher goes over the material with five different sets of students. By the time she gets to the fifth group, she may no longer remember exactly which items she's already mentioned.

Your child should make certain he knows which type of test is being given. He may want to prepare differently for an essay test than he would for a true-false test. On an essay test, it would be most important to make certain that he understands all the broad concepts and perhaps has memorized a couple of quotes that would make the essay sound more official. For a true-false test covering the same material, he'd want to concentrate more on the factual details of his studies.

THE TRUTH ABOUT STANDARDIZED TESTS

Recently, a mother lamented, "It seems to me that my son is always taking some kind of standardized something or other. Sometimes, I think my child's whole future is going to be determined by the little circles he blackens in boxes on standardized tests. Worse still, I don't even understand what the difference is in half the tests he has to take."

Parents often suffer from a kind of test anxiety of their own. Part of that is because you care about your child and want him to do well. However, a good deal of parental anxiety about standardized testing seems to stem from the educational jargon that accompanies it. This section is devoted to explaining in simple terms some of the most common types of standardized tests and showing you some reasons why the tests are taken by your child as well as what the results mean.

Just exactly what are standardized tests? By definition, they're examinations that are always scored the same way, are given with an allotted time limit, and have a factual, agreed upon answer for each question. Standardized tests have been constructed by a group of individuals that usually include specially trained test technicians. Construction of the test is a time-consuming and involved process that includes evaluating the content of the test, evaluating the readability of the questions, and a process of first pretesting and then reevaluating each item before the test is put into actual use.

Standardized tests are not a substitute for teacher-made tests in the classroom. Schools give standardized tests to be able to measure groups of students' performances against the performance of other groups of students not only in the same school but all across the country. Because different teachers have different expectations for their students, one teacher's requirements for an A might be very different than another's, and so standardized tests serve an important role. They not only help you know where your child stands in relation to other children his age and grade but they help schools see if their programs are succeeding.

The Aptitude Test

Perhaps you've heard a proud parent boast that his child has a very high IQ and you've felt bad because you know that your own child has an IQ that's just in the average range. Well, hold on! IQ scores are unfortunately bandied around much too freely and are looked at as being absolutes while actually they are not intended to be anything more than guidelines. The term IQ stands for *intelligence quotient* and it is most often determined by a particular kind of aptitude test.

The IQ test has been developed to show a child's mental age. This is determined by answers to questions given on specific tests. Each IQ test is normed according to a large population, and charts based on the norm are provided to the test giver. She uses these charts to score a child's answers and assign him an IQ. In the United States, an intelligence quotient of below 70 is considered retarded, 80 to 90 is classified below average, 90 to 110 is average and over 110 is considered above average. In many school districts around the country, an IQ of 130 or higher is necessary to qualify for gifted programs. However, and I cannot stress this however enough, IQ is only one measure of intelligence. An IQ test can be influenced by a person's feeling upset, nervous, or ill when he takes the test. IQ tests are used to help parents and teachers make realistic consider-ations concerning a child's ability, but they are only one measure of that ability. A high score on an aptitude test does not ensure auto-matic academic success, nor does an average score mean that a child may not be a fine student. Some research has shown that there may be as many as 144 different components of intelligence; the test your child is taking may measure as few as fourteen. Thus, the IQ score is an indicator, nothing more.

There are several different types of aptitude tests. Some must be administered individually and some are group tests. Two of the most common individual tests are the Stanford-Binet Intelligence Scale and the Wechsler Scales. The administration of either of these tests requires a qualified examiner who has been trained in how to give the exam and interpret the results. Because of the amount of time it takes to administer these tests, and the cost to the school district, these tests are not usually given to large groups of students. Instead, they are usually only used when there is some special reason for wanting to carefully measure the mental ability of a child.

Group aptitude tests cover a wide range of items from a single academic area to a broad base. For example, the Lee-Clark Reading Readiness Test helps teachers determine whether students who are entering first grade are ready for reading instruction. The Otis Quick-Scoring Mental Ability Tests sample a variety of mental traits and have one test for grades 1 through 4, one for grades 5 through 9, and another test for high school and college students. Other test names you may hear in connection with aptitude testing are the California Test of Mental Maturity (CTMM) and the School and Col-lege Ability Tests (SCAT).

On the following page are some sample aptitude-test questions.

Again, let me stress that you should not look at any one aptitude test as an absolute determiner of your child's ability. Such tests can only predict the likelihood of a student's future success in school as compared to other students. Scores on aptitude tests can be affected by past achievement, and they are probably of more use in elemen-tary school than high school.

EXAMPLES OF INDIVIDUAL ABILITIES TEST ITEMS

Age 8

Verbal Reasoning Area

Absurdities Test:
The examinee might be shown a picture of a child smashing a tennis ball across the net, but the child's tennis racket has a hole in it larger than the size of a tennis ball. The examinee is asked what is silly/wrong about the picture.

Comprehension Test:
The examinee might be asked: "Why should cars stop when they are following a school bus that has stopped to pick up riders?"

Quantitative Reasoning Area

Number Series Test:
The examinee might be asked which two numbers would come next in the following series: 7, 10, 13, 16, 19, __, __

Short-Term Memory Area

Memory for Sentences Test:
The examinee might be asked to repeat the following sentence: "Mary asked Joe if he would mail a letter for her."

Age 12

Verbal Reasoning Area

Absurdities Test:
The examinee might be shown a picture of the sun setting at dusk. Everything in the picture looks normal except that the sun is setting in the east. The examinee is asked what is silly/wrong about the picture.

Comprehension Test:
The examinee might be asked: "Give two reasons why some people would rather drive than fly to a location."

Quantitative Reasoning Area

Number Series Test:
The examinee might be asked which two numbers would come next in the following series: 5, 7, 4, 8, 3, __, __

Short-Term Memory Area

Memory for Sentences Test:
The examinee might be asked to repeat the following sentence: "The family was enjoying their stay at the campgrounds until it started raining."

While not actual test items, these items were provided by The Riverside Publishing Company as examples of the kinds of items that are used in the Fourth Edition of the Stanford-Binet Intelligence Scale.

Achievement Tests

The major difference between aptitude and achievement tests is that while aptitude is measuring what your child might be *capable* of learning, achievement tests measure how well he understands what he has already been taught. Your child will probably take more achievement tests than any other type of standardized test while he is in school. These tests show how much your child has learned about such subjects as reading, mathematics, language, spelling, social studies, and science compared to other children in his grade.

Standardized achievement tests can be used to let a teacher see areas where her program might need to be emphasized and to give a principal and school district an opportunity to plan their goals and curriculum. Along with other measures, standardized achievement tests are also used to help determine those children who need special help.

Some of the most common standardized achievement tests are the CAT (California Achievement Tests), Iowa Tests of Basic Skills, Stanford Achievement Tests, and MAT (Metropolitan Achievement Tests). Below are sample achievement-test questions.

EXAMPLES OF STANDARDIZED TEST ITEMS

Grade 3—Reading Comprehension

1) What is the main idea in this passage?

   A. Carol enjoys playing at Sharon's house on Saturdays.
   B. Carol likes to help her father at home.
   C. Carol would rather stay at home than visit friends.
   D. Carol likes to play with her brothers and sisters.

2) What is the poet doing?

   A. Running in a race
   B. Watching a race

   C. Describing an event at a track meet
   D. Imagining winning a race

* *About half of the students answer these types of items correctly.*

Grade 3—Mathematics Concepts

1) Which number is less than 8?
   A. 7
   B. 9
   C. 10
   D. 8

   * *Almost all students answer this type of item correctly.*

2) How do you write $300 + 60 + 7$ as one numeral?
   A. 367
   B. 900
   C. 30607
   D. 3607

* *About half of the students answer this type of item correctly.*

Grade 3—Mathematics Computation

1) $9 \times 7 =$

   A. 63
   B. 16
   C. 2
   D. N
          (N means Not Given)

   * *About half of the students answer this type of item correctly.*

2)   9
    $\underline{+3}$

A. 93
B. 12
C. 6
D. N

* *Almost all students answer this type of item correctly.*

The above items are not from any specific test but closely resemble those in the Iowa Tests of Basic Skills and were provided courtesy of The Riverside Publishing Company.

Grade 6—Reading Comprehension

1) Which of the following words best describes Andrew?

    A. Discouraged
    B. Modest
    C. Proud
    D. Elated

* *About three fourths of the students answer this type of item correctly.*

2) Which paragraphs describe the parade?
    A. 2 and 3
    B. 2, 3, and 4
    C. 2, 5, and 6
    D. 4, 5, and 6

* *About one third of the students answer this type of item correctly.*

Grade 6—Mathematics Concepts

1) What fraction has a denominator of 3?

    A. $\dfrac{1}{4}$

    B. $\dfrac{5}{7}$

C. $\frac{1}{3}$

D. $6\frac{1}{8}$

* *About three fourths of the students answer this type of item correctly.*

2) Which gives the best estimate of $5.95 \times 12\frac{9}{11}$?

A. 6×13
B. 5×13
C. 6×12
D. 5×12

* *About one third of the students answer this type of item correctly.*

Grade 6—Mathematics Computation

1)   632
    $-$ 74

A. 558
B. 568
C. 708
D. N

* *About three fourths of the students answer this type of item correctly.*

2) $\frac{1}{4}$
   $\times 9$

A. $\frac{1}{36}$

B. $2\frac{1}{4}$

C. 30

D. N

** About one fourth of the students answer this type of item
correctly.*

*The above items are not from any specific test, but closely resemble
those in the Iowa Tests of Basic Skills and were provided courtesy
of The Riverside Publishing Company.*

UNDERSTANDING THE TERMINOLOGY OF TESTS

"Johnny just finished taking the CAT, and you can see that on
this norm-referenced test, his raw score, percentile rank, stanine,
and grade equivalent make it clear as to his basic achievement
strengths and weaknesses."

If you've just read the above paragraph and felt totally confused
about what it said, you're probably not alone. When your child
comes home with his results from a standardized test, don't be
intimidated by all the terminology. You have a right and a responsibility to fully understand what the various test scores mean. Actually, that becomes a much easier task once the terminology is
translated from educationalese to simple English. Below you will
find that translation. Review it before you go through your child's
test scores, and you will probably find that they make more sense.
However, if at any time you become concerned or confused about
the standardized test results that have been sent home, you should
definitely make an appointment and have a teacher or administrator
give you a full explanation.

Testing Terminology

Norm-referenced test—A norm-referenced test measures broad
skills of learning, and each student who takes the test is compared
with a large sample upon which reliability and validity studies have
been done.

It is one of the few opportunities for you to see how your child is
doing not just in comparison to his classmates or the rest of his
school, but in the case of most nationally standardized norm-

referenced tests, how he is doing in comparison to the other children in his grade across the country. (This type of test is different from a criterion-referenced test which we will talk about later.)

Raw scores—The reason the term is called raw score is that it's usually the number of total questions your child answered correctly. It doesn't break down which questions were missed or in what areas. By itself this score doesn't have much meaning, and you needn't be too concerned with it.

Percentile—This is a term that tells what percent of a norm group scored lower than your child. For example, if your son comes home with an 80 percentile score in math concepts, it means that 80 percent of the norm group who took the test scored lower than your child did on the test. In actuality, your son may have only answered half of the total questions on the test, but that was more correct answers than 80 percent of the other children scored on the test. Parents become confused when they don't understand that percentile and percent mean two different things. An 80 percentile score on a standardized test does *not* mean that your child answered 80 percent of the questions correctly. It only means that he scored better than 80 percent of the total norm-referenced group and that 20 percent of the children across the nation who took this test scored better than he. An 80 percent score means that he got 80 percent of the items correct.

Stanine—A stanine is a more general measure than a percentile score. Stanine scores go from one to nine, and each stanine score includes several percentile scores. For example, a stanine of 5 includes all students who scored a percentile between 60 and 40.

The most important thing to remember when examining your child's test score is that stanine scores of 1, 2, and 3 are well below the average scores of other children who took the test. A stanine score of 4 is slightly below average, 5 is average, 6 is slightly above average, and 7, 8, and 9 show that your child scored well above the average scores of other children.

Grade Equivalents—This is expressed in a number like 5.2, which means fifth grade, second month. The score represents the average grade level of other students across the nation who scored the same as your child. IT DOESN'T TELL YOU WHAT GRADE YOUR CHILD SHOULD BE IN. For example, if your third grader scored 5.2, it shows only that he scored as well as an average fifth grader would score on the third-grade test. Though it means his work is well above average for a third grader, it does not mean that he could do fifth-grade work or that he should be skipped into fifth grade. It may indicate that your child should be getting some enrichment and should be working in the top groups in the third grade. By the same token, if he scores 2.0, it doesn't mean that he should automatically be retained. It may indicate, however, that the child is having trouble and needs some extra help. Grade equivalent is frequently used in explaining test results because it is terminology which parents understand; however, stanines are actually a more accurate interpretation of results.

Most of the standardized achievement tests given compare your child to a national group, and his school may choose to send home further documentation and figures showing grade level and percentiles in terms of how the students in his grade in his school did. This may be interesting to you because these are the children with whom he works every day. He may be above the national average and still feeling frustrated because most of the children in his grade are even higher above the national average.

Understanding the terminology of testing can help you get an accurate picture of what all the numbers are that your child is bringing home. You certainly should feel very comfortable in making an appointment with a teacher or a principal if any aspect of your child's scores concern you. You don't have to wait for the school to contact you. The large numbers in the school system may mean that only the parents whose children's scores reflect the possibility of great problems may be contacted, so you may find that if you do have a question, once you begin talking with the teacher, she'll tell you that she's glad you got in touch with her.

The school will usually notify all parents to let them know when standardized testing will take place and there are several things that you, as a parent, can do to help your child achieve his best. Make certain that he gets enough sleep before the test, and that he eats a good breakfast before he goes to school. Let your child know that you hope he will try to do his best on the test. One third grader began going through his test answer sheet filling in the blanks so that they made a pretty picture. When his teacher noticed and asked the boy what he was doing, the child shrugged, "My mom said this doesn't count on our grade, and I didn't feel like taking a test today."

On the other hand, avoid putting undue pressure on your child. One parent that I know of sat his child down before the tests this year and showed him his older sister's scores from the year before. "See how well your sister did," he said, "and your grades have been better than hers this year, so I know you'll do really well on these tests. Don't let us down now, okay!" I'm sure that the parent only thought that he was giving his child a good pep talk and reassuring him that he could do well on the test; however, in actuality, he raised his son's test anxiety to such a degree that the child couldn't think clearly.

There is always a possible measure of error on the test: For example, one student stays up so late the night before the test that he can barely stay awake during it and thus scores poorly while another student happens to make enough lucky guesses to push his score higher than it should be. These kinds of individual errors make the test more valid when it is looked at in terms of the group scores. Various individual scores are balanced within the group.

If the school is making an evaluation of your child, it should include not only standardized test scores, but teacher observation of the child, evaluation of the child's day-to-day classwork and tests, and teacher and parent communication with the child.

ALL ABOUT CRITERION-REFERENCED TESTS

Most standardized tests are norm-referenced. That is, they measure your child against all the children who took the test to determine the excellence of his performance. However, during the course of his schooling, your child will also take criterion-referenced achievement tests. These are frequently used as diagnostic tests. At the beginning of a unit or sometimes the start of a school year, a teacher will give a test designed to measure certain skills. A math teacher might write a test with a section of problems that assess whether the child can add multiple-digit numbers, work story problems, and subtract single-digit numbers. The teacher then grades these tests for each area, noting the number right. A certain percentage correct is necessary for the child to achieve mastery of the concept. In other words, achievement is based only on whether the skill has been mastered, not on how other students do. This kind of test is helpful to teachers in knowing where to place students in groups, and what areas to emphasize in their teaching. Based on the example above, the teacher may decide that Sandy's scores mean she needs to be in a math group that will work hard to review addition, Jared may need to be in a group that's working on subtraction, and Linda may be able to be put in a math group that is working on writing its own story problems for addition and subtraction.

A criterion-referenced test may be given again at a later date to determine whether each student has achieved the skill or concept that was taught. Unlike norm-referenced tests in which items vary in difficulty, and discriminate between high and low achievers, the items on a criterion-referenced test measure specific rather than broad characteristics and all learners are aiming to achieve mastery.

While a norm-referenced test may state only that your child's math is the grade equivalent of 2.3, the criterion-referenced test will state that he has or has not mastered subtraction of numbers between 1 and 10.

MINIMUM-COMPETENCY TESTING

In some cities and states the concern that it is possible for a student to graduate from high school without basic skills has created a desire for minimum-competency testing. Depending on the school district, your child may have to take no competency test, one every so many grades, or several each year. The idea behind giving competency tests is that if students don't do well on them, they can be given special help and the problem can be corrected before it gets worse. You might ask your school principal if minimum-competency tests are given and, if so, in which grades. If he says that they are given, you should make certain that you know what will happen if your child does not pass the competency test. If you are interested in this area of testing, you can get more detailed information and models of how various states are handling minimum-competency testing by reading a Phi Delta Kappa Fastback booklet entitled *Minimum Competency Testing,* by Rodney P. Riegle and Ned B. Lovell.

INTEREST INVENTORIES

Your child may also have the opportunity to take some tests that will help him decide on an eventual career he might like to pursue. One of the most common is the Kuder Preference. The idea of these interest inventories is to relate the child's interest to occupations. Because a child normally only considers a narrow range of possible occupations, these interest inventories may help him think about occupations he might enjoy that he would otherwise never have considered. Parents are usually quite interested and sometimes quite surprised to see what kinds of things their children show as high interests. It is wise, however, to remember that these surveys do not in any way measure ability. So it may be suggested that a student who measures a high science interest consider a job as a biochemist; however, this may not be realistic if his science grades in school have always been low.

COLLEGE-ENTRANCE EXAMINATIONS

Most four-year colleges and universities require your child to take and submit the scores from either the SAT (Scholastic Aptitude

Test) or the ACT (American College Testing Program) when he applies for admission. The literature for these tests says that they are devices to help your son or daughter in selecting a college that meets his needs and to help the college choose students who meet its standards.

The SAT is a test that concentrates less on a student's factual knowledge and more on his ability. It is divided into two sections: Verbal, which includes the ability to read with understanding and reason with words, and Math, which shows the student's aptitude in solving math problems and stresses math reasoning. Students score between 200 and 800. Statistically, about two thirds of those who take the test score between 400 and 600.

Along with the SAT, which is most often taken by seniors in high school, is the PSAT (Preliminary Scholastic Aptitude Test) which is geared for juniors and gives students a chance to practice for the SAT and set realistic college plans.

The ACT is structured slightly differently. It tests in English, social studies, math, and science. Students receive a test score on each section as well as an overall composite score. There are books available as well as computer software to let students practice taking sample college-entrance tests.

Testing is an important part of school, and learning some basic test-taking skills is really not that hard to do. Imagine how good it will make your child feel to look at a test and know he has a secret weapon to attack it with success—he has the test-wise tips you've taught him.

SEVEN

WHAT TO DO WHEN YOUR CHILD IS HAVING ACADEMIC OR BEHAVIOR PROBLEMS

Liz checked her sleeping child and smiled. He looked so vulnerable and so sweet. Then she sighed, thinking of his not-so-sweet report card and wishing that somehow its grades would magically improve. The D's and F's clearly spelled failure. Liz couldn't help it. Her eyes filled with tears, and her heart ached with worry over what kind of future her son would have. She ran her hand nervously through her hair and wondered how everything could have gone so very wrong.

If ever there should be a natural basis for parent-teacher cooperation and communication it should be in dealing with the child who is having academic or behavior problems. After all, what parent wants his child to fail, and what teacher wants her students to be confused or disruptive? Yet unfortunately it seems no area is more frequently treacherous for all involved. Worried parents and defensive teachers often miscommunicate totally, with the unhappy result being that children continue to fail. It doesn't have to be that

138

way, but it may well be up to you to make certain that it isn't. Just what should you do if your child begins having academic or discipline problems?

WHAT EXACTLY IS THE PROBLEM?

Perhaps the first thing you need to work out is whether your child is having academic problems because of his behavior or the other way around. Consider two sophomore high school students who both received a D − in English and an unsatisfactory in behavior. From the teacher's perspective, both boys tended to turn in sketchy, unfinished assignments, and neither seemed to pay much attention in class. Both were frequently ready with some smart comment whenever they were called upon, and both seemed to be relatively well liked by their peers. The two sound like clones, right? The teacher who had the two boys only fifty minutes a day was rather confused herself for a while, but there were actually some very great differences between the two.

Bob knew he was in over his head. He'd tried to hint to his parents that he needed to go into a different class; however, they'd never picked up on the hints. Bob decided that they'd been so proud of his being selected for this advanced English class that he'd be letting them down if he came right out and said he needed to go into a regular class. He began to hate English; it made him feel as if his friends were going to start calling him stupid, until he figured out a way to fix things. Instead of hanging his head when he didn't know an answer, he raised his hand and volunteered something funny. Soon his classmates thought him a great wit; the teacher was ready to kill him, but no one had any idea that he was covering up a growing sense of confusion.

Greg, on the other hand, could have done the work and done it well. Sometimes he thought it would be very nice to get good grades, but when it came right down to it, it simply wasn't worth the trouble. Giving the right answer in class was boring; giving the wrong answer got a lot of laughs. Furthermore, it was a pain to do homework. Playing basketball with the guys, watching TV with friends, working on the car he was trying to restore—those things were fun. Besides, he had a reputation to keep. Everyone knew that Greg was the guy to be around when you were ready to have fun. Laziness, poor study habits, and enjoyment of his role as a "party guy" were responsible for Greg's poor grades.

Bob didn't have the academic ability to be in the particular group in which he'd been placed. Stress and pressure had created a classic student solution that goes, "If you can't be the smartest, you sure can be the funniest." Greg had a tremendous academic aptitude; he had a behavior and attitude problem that made him shrug, "Somehow it'll all work out, and I don't care as long as I'm having fun." In Bob's case, the solution to the trouble came in getting him in the right academic setting while maintaining a positive self-image about the change. In Greg's situation, the solution came in having his parents and teachers work together to establish a standard of behavior to which he had to adhere. The solution for one of these boys was not at all the same as the answer for the other even though on the surface both boys appeared to be so much alike.

No parent is very pleased to see his child bring home a report card with D's or F's. However, the first thing a parent must do is try to get to the bottom of why the grades are bad. Behavior problems that are caused by academic failure usually disappear once the child gets help with academics. Academic failure caused by behavior problems, however, will not be solved by getting academic help; in fact, usually the behavior gets even worse and the grades will continue to stay poor.

So how do you tell the difference? Here are several suggestions.

- Talk to your child. Let him know that you are quite concerned about him, but don't dwell on his report card grades. They're finished; he can't change those particular marks. The parent who opens a report card envelope and screams at his child that the child is grounded for the next month hasn't gotten very far in knowing *why* the child got those grades.

Tell your child that you want to work with him and his teacher to make school more successful. Let the child know that you're on his side. This will make him much more likely to tell you if he is having academic trouble. In the years I've taught, I've seen kids go as far as getting themselves kicked out of school before letting their parents know that their academic abilities are not what the parents had hoped for. They decide that it's better to make their parents think they're juvenile delinquents rather than disappoint them with the knowledge that they've got a child who isn't "good enough."

You and your child should work out a definite plan for improving his grades and write it out. This is reassuring to the child who is having academic problems. He can see positive action that will help him out of what may seem like a hopeless mess to him. Writing a definite plan also works to corral a child with a discipline problem. With a concrete study plan and frequent monitoring, he soon finds out that he can't get away with doing nothing, so he might as well be in a higher group and have the work be more interesting.

- Make an appointment to talk to the child's teacher or teachers. Explain that you are concerned both about the behavior and the academic problems, and while you want to get both solved, you wonder if the teacher could help you in figuring out which one is causing the other. If your child has returned assignments at home, bring some of them in to go over with the teacher. Make it clear that you're not trying to get his grade changed on any of them, you'd just like the teacher's expertise on whether your child could or couldn't have done the work better. Try to ask the teacher specific questions. For example, you might ask your child's English teacher whether he is having more trouble in grammar, vocabulary, reading, writing, or if he is equally confused in everything.

- Speak to his counselor or a school individual who can review your child's standardized achievement and aptitude tests with you. What do those tests show? In general, how does your child compare to others in his grade?

- Pull out old report cards and reread comments from previous teachers. What kind of a pattern is developing from them? Did the first few speak primarily of some trouble understanding the material or did they address the concern of lack of effort?

Once you've had a chance to go over all the results of these questions, you'll probably have a pretty good idea of whether the basic problem is academic or behavioral in nature. However, knowing is only the first step. The next problem is what do you do about it?

Academic problems need to be broken down more specifically in order to deal with them. Is your child having trouble in just one subject or are there problems in all areas? Is this a very temporary thing or have his troubles been getting greater each year? Is your child in first grade or tenth?

THE SYMPTOMS OF ACADEMIC TROUBLE

You don't have to wait for a bad report card or a phone call from a teacher to have a pretty good idea as to when your child is having academic trouble. Head the problem off from the top. Be aware of some symptoms of sudden academic trouble.

- A sudden interest in watching more television. Escaping inside the television set is an easy way for a child to remove himself from thinking about or dealing with the problems he is having at school.

- A newfound reluctance to go to school. Any time your child suddenly starts saying that he doesn't want to go to school, you can be fairly certain that there is something really bothering him there which he either doesn't know how to cope with or thinks he cannot handle. Sometimes it's a social problem; sometimes it's an academic problem, but it is always worth further investigation on your part.

- Complaints about distractions in the classroom. His seat hasn't been changed, but recently your child has begun to complain that he can't think because the kids who sit around him are always talking. The teacher is the same one he thought was fine a few weeks ago, but he now complains that she is always getting off the subject. You get the idea. As the child begins to have academic problems in the classroom, he starts looking for scapegoat reasons upon which to blame them. Be alert to this. You can't help your child solve his academic problems until you can help him face them. The child who always pins the blame on something or someone else has no reason to change himself.

- Headaches and stomachaches. Stress and tension are not limited to adults. Children who sense failure feel tremendous tension that frequently lets itself out in the form of headaches and stomachaches. If your child has begun complaining of one or both, you certainly may want to take him to a physician for a checkup, but you're missing an important step if you don't also check with your child's teacher to see if your child has begun experiencing problems in school. Even if the teacher doesn't think he has, it doesn't mean it isn't happening. It may just be too soon yet for her to see the consequences of his growing confusion.

- Comments in which the child expresses the idea that he never really did think he was going to be much good at school. This is a defense system that he is setting up so that failure doesn't hurt so much. Don't brush him off by saying, "Of course you're going to be fine. You're very capable." This may seem like reassurance to you, but it could well make your child retreat further into his shell, feeling as if you don't understand and he has no ally to whom he can turn. Instead of striving for instant reassurance, try to ascertain the reasons he feels he can't succeed. Working with your child to find solutions to his problems is far more valuable than patting him on the head and saying that things will get better. If you decide you need to boost his ego, try to do so by supporting his specific successes.

LEVEL LEARNING

Part of your investigation of your child's academic problems should include finding out what level he is in. Most elementary schools have leveled groups; in fact, you may well remember being in such reading groups as The Reds, The Blues, and The Greens, or The Rockets, The Stars, and The Suns. The idea is that by not labeling the groups one, two, and three, children won't know who is in the top or the bottom reading group. However, I'm convinced that they know exactly; the only ones who are confused are the parents. Sometimes solving academic problems can be as simple as requesting an adjustment in your child's reading or math group.

Why don't teachers automatically do this? One confided, "I never have any trouble moving a child up into a higher group, but I'm so tired of arguing with parents when I have to move a child down a group, that I just don't do it if I think the child can even marginally survive in the higher group." Other times, teachers are not aware of the frustration or time at home that a child is putting in to stay in a particular group. Whatever the reason, if you suspect that your child is in the wrong group, make an appointment and talk to the teacher.

In junior high and high school there are many honors classes. The idea of these classes is to keep a bright child challenged and motivated to learn. For an average child who was working hard already, an accelerated class can be a most frustrating experience. Yet these kids often put tremendous pressure on themselves, as do their parents, to stay in the class. Recently, I suggested to a father that I felt his child was working too hard in an advanced English class to be barely passing. "I'm recommending that he be moved down a level," I said. "School should be a successful experience, and there is no reason Rory should be put in a situation where he's working this hard and getting such poor results."

The father's voice shook with fury. "I suppose I can't stop you from moving him down, but if my son doesn't get into medical school, it will be your fault!"

FAILING FIRST GRADE

Nothing is more devastating to a parent than to be told that the school wants to flunk his five- or six-year-old. Said one mother, "I felt like such a failure. How could my Missy be so smart until she got to school and then flunk. I don't know whether I should let them hold her back."

It's easy to understand why a parent would be upset, but before you automatically reject retention or consider yourself or your child a failure, try to clear away the emotionalism enough to hear what is being said and decide logically how to act upon it. First, realize that if a child needs to be retained, it is best to do so at the youngest possible age. The older the child, the less likely that retention will improve his performance, so don't figure that you'll push him on now, and if things are still this bad at the end of next year, you'll hold him back then.

Second, go over standardized norm- and criterion-referenced tests given to your child. Consult with the school professionals in interpretation of the tests if necessary. If a learning or physical disability is suspected, insist on further testing to pinpoint the problem. If the results of the tests show that a physical handicap or a learning disability is the primary cause of his school problems, it is unwise to retain your child. He needs to get special help but to be kept on grade level. Merely retaining him will not solve his academic problems; it will only take him away from his peer group.

If after studying all the material and consulting with school officials you all feel that the problem is developmental, by all means let the school retain the child. It is the biggest favor you can do for him in terms of academic success. Some of the indicators may include your child still having trouble holding on to a pencil, following directions, or sitting still. These spell trouble in first grade. Give him another year to mature and the problems will take care of themselves. After all, starting kindergarten at five and first grade at six are arbitrary cut-offs. Not every child matures and develops at exactly the same rate. Sue Cohen, a veteran kindergarten teacher, said, shaking her head sadly, "So often, when I suggest another year of kindergarten to a parent, the parent acts as if I've destroyed him and his child. The parent insists on pushing the child onward and then the child has tremendous academic problems in first grade. It could all have been avoided if parental ego didn't prevent giving the child a little longer to mature. The child who reads at three and the child who reads at seven may be equally good readers by the time they are both eleven."

Your child will need your support if he is to be retained successfully. If he feels that you are upset about it, he'll feel as if he's failed. Not only that, but you may need to stress the positives to counteract his little friends saying, "Mike failed—Mike's a dummy." Help him protect his self-image by explaining that he's one of the younger kids in his class and by going to kindergarten again, he'll have friends more his own age. You might tell him that you heard there were going to be some wonderful new projects being done in kin′ dergarten next year, and you didn't want him to have to miss them. If you cannot escape your child's being ridiculed or his image of defeat at being held back, you might consider changing schools for your child. In this way, none of the other children will know whether he has or hasn't been retained.

IT'S A PHYSICAL PROBLEM

Andrew was having both behavior and academic problems, but no one could pin down why. A routine hearing screening provided by a volunteer parent provided the first clue. She told the school nurse, "Andrew says he has no hearing problems, but I can't get any response from him on his right side." The nurse checked Andrew's ears and immediately called his mother, suggesting that she take him to a doctor as soon as possible because it looked to her as if there might be a tumor in his ear. Her astute diagnosis proved correct, and the tumor, which turned out to be malignant, was caught in time and successfully removed. The amazing thing was that though the child had totally lost his hearing on the right side, he'd never mentioned it, nor had anyone else become aware of it.

Often diagnosing physical problems is just the beginning of improving school performance. A hearing aid cannot help a child if the batteries are dead. Glasses that are in a child's pocket instead of on his face will not help him in seeing the board. Parents need to work with children to give them a positive attitude about using any aids that exist to help them. They need to inform teachers so that teachers can be aware of what to watch for. I really appreciated the mother who took a moment to contact me saying, "Please don't tell Kim I called, but she just got glasses, and I'm afraid she won't wear them at school because she thinks they make her look ugly." I made a point of complimenting Kim on how the blue in the frames really made her eyes blue, and a week later, I called the mother back to reassure her that Kim was, indeed, wearing the glasses. A simple matter of parent-teacher teamwork that was very unlike the student I had with a hearing handicap. I seated students alphabetically and this girl's last name meant she sat in the very back of the class. It wasn't until the last week of school when I complimented her on a paper that she'd written that she told me, "Yeah, I think I would have done better in here, but I have this thing they call an auditory-discrimination problem and I need to sit in a front seat or I can't screen out other noises." Why hadn't the mother or the child told me at the beginning of the year? She'd been cheated out of getting the most from her education.

The schools will work with you if you work with them. One last story shows just how that cooperation can succeed. A boy was being teased about his hearing aid and wouldn't wear it. At wit's end, his parents scheduled a conference with the child's teacher, principal, and coordinator of special education. They arrived at the idea of a hearing aid that looked like a Sony Walkman. Suddenly, he was the envy of every kid at school who wished they could wear a radio/headphone like his.

There are many types of physical disabilities that a child may face. Today's schools are sensitive to them. Please check with your school to find out about the programs that could best help your child.

Finally, one last health problem that can be corrected easily. Your child can't learn adequately if he's too tired or too hungry. Please see that your child eats properly and goes to bed at a reasonable hour each night. That information doesn't just apply to small children. I have teenage girls on fad diets who are so hungry their concentration powers are practically nil. I have students who work from late afternoon until midnight every night, and I watch as their eyelids flutter open and shut while they try to stay awake during school.

MAYBE MY CHILD HAS A LEARNING DISABILITY

Jill was a college-educated mother who was used to handling most situations well, but her world collapsed around her when she was called in to the conference concerning her son's special-education testing. In the back of her mind, she'd been so sure that somehow things would just work out. Now they were talking about her Joey, her perfect boy, having a learning disability. She fought back tears, "He's not retarded. I know he's not."

She was right. He wasn't mentally retarded. No one said he was, but part of the problem in improving academic achievement for children with learning disabilities is getting past labels to provide the help that is needed. A learning-disabled child may be very bright in some areas, but he has at least one weakness that keeps him from performing well academically.

In the next chapter we'll talk about the testing process for entering a special-education program under information about the school psychologist, and we'll talk about the kinds of services the special-education teacher can provide. It's important that you don't rule out available assistance just because you don't want to see your child labeled. How frustrating it is for the school to offer the service, the child to suffer because he cannot do the work without the extra help, and the parent to refuse to let the help happen.

However, for even the most cooperative, supportive parent there remains another problem. Not all learning-disabled children qualify for any sort of special program. As one psychologist told me, "Every human being probably has some degree of a learning disability somewhere." For many programs the child has to lag two or more years behind his grade level in order to qualify. So if you suspect problems, but your child is not severe enough to fit into any program, you can still get help. You'll simply have to turn to outside sources.

WHAT ABOUT TUTORING?

Before you hire someone to tutor your child, check to see if his regular teacher has after-school help sessions and ask whether the school has a peer-tutoring program. While these possibilities do not occur everywhere, and while they certainly don't work for every child, because they are no-cost, no-travel alternatives they are definitely worth investigating.

If you do decide to hire a tutor for your child, you should carefully evaluate the individual before hiring her. One mother selected her child's tutor out of an ad in the paper, saying, "I'm so grateful to find someone to help my daughter with her math, and the tutor only lives a couple of blocks from my house."

This mother had simply assumed that because the woman had advertised herself as a qualified math tutor, she must be good. Yet having worked with and watched various tutors over the years, I can testify to the fact that some are excellent and some are a waste of money and time. Check the credentials of anyone you hire to help your child. You may want to begin your search by asking the school for recommendations, and then ask the prospective tutor if you could speak to some of the parents whose children have been tu-tored by her. Check the facility in which your child will be tutored. Many people tutor out of their homes, which is fine, but it is impor-tant to ask how the tutor handles phone calls during tutoring time, and if she has children, whether they will be coming home during the tutoring session. Where will the tutoring be done? Is it a quiet place with study supplies and room enough for the tutor and child to work together?

Before hiring her, tell the tutor as much as you know about your child's academic problem. Ask her how she thinks she can help him. Listen carefully, and if you don't think you understand her, ask again.

Make certain that the tutor plans to check with the regular class-room teacher, and ask her if you get a copy of the child's regular textbook whether she'd be willing to use it. Ask her if she would talk to your child's teacher to see what they are doing in the classroom and how to best coordinate her tutoring to improve his classroom skill.

Tutoring today has become big business. The Reading Game and Sylvan Learning Centers are just two of the national concerns that have entered many local marketplaces. They offer impressive statis-tics about both the number of children they have helped and the extent of that help, but don't make your decision by statistics alone. Ask to observe the tutoring and to look at their materials before making a decision. These centers offer customized instruction in reading, math, and study skills after giving the child a battery of tests to determine areas of weakness. They guarantee a ratio of no more than three children to one teacher. Both of these programs try to stimulate the children to pay attention by offering "good effort" tokens which may be traded at the school "store" for prizes that are on display. Such a setup may be exactly what your child needs, but since these programs run more than $20 an hour, you may instead be able to find a good tutor for a fraction of what they cost. The bottom line is that getting a little additional help at the right time may make all the difference in your child's academic improvement and image of himself, but simply hiring any tutor doesn't assure that. You must be involved in whom you hire initially, you must monitor the progress or lack of it, and you must have the cooperation of your child. If your child is not a willing participant in the tutoring process, chances are you are wasting your money, so it's a good idea to discuss the idea before you hire any tutor. Present tutoring in a positive way, explaining that it may make schoolwork much easier to handle. Listen to the child's possible objections, and try to overcome them before you start the tutoring process.

THEY SAY MY CHILD'S A DISCIPLINE PROBLEM

"Bryan can do the work, he simply won't. He's failed to turn in ten of the last twelve assignments."

"Gary is the class clown. Yesterday he caught a fly and ate it to amuse his classmates. I am not amused. He must stop disrupting class."

"Gina was truant from her biology class yesterday. She was found smoking a cigarette in the parking lot of the convenience market across the street from school."

"Sandy hit the girl sitting in back of her yesterday. She said the girl took her pen."

"Allan is being sent home for wearing a T-shirt saying 'I'm a sex stud' on the front of it. He was asked to finish the day by wearing the T-shirt inside out and then not to wear it again. He refused. Please do not allow him to come to school dressed inappropriately in the future."

These discipline reports taken from the files of school principals and deans show just a few of the everyday behavior problems which the school must handle. How would you have responded if your child had been the one involved? Would it have been as any of these parents did?

Bryan's mother shook her head in defeat. "I don't know what to do with him," she said. "Every night I yell at him to do his homework; every night he ignores me. I keep telling him he's going to grow up to be a bum just like his uncle, but he doesn't pay me any mind. What can I do?"

Gina's mother complained about the school's no-smoking policy. "Gina's a nervous girl; she knows she shouldn't smoke, but it calms her nerves. If there were a place at the school where the kids could smoke, she wouldn't have had to go to the convenience store."

Sandy's mother came to school immediately after the principal called. Sandy was waiting in the principal's office. Her mother listened carefully to the story of what happened and when the principal had finished explaining, she turned to Sandy. "Is that true?" Sandy nodded yes. The mother rose from her seat and slapped Sandy across the face. "You're ten years old. You're too old to be hitting kids," she told the crying child.

Allan's father threatened to sue the school. "Haven't you people ever heard of freedom of expression?" he asked angrily. "My son's a healthy sixteen-year-old boy. I don't see what's wrong with his letting people know it."

Needless to say, none of these parents did much to solve his children's discipline problems or to assure them less chance of future trouble in school. In fact, in different ways, each parent reinforced the child's negative behavior. Yet I don't believe that any of these parents intended to have that effect. I think most parents want their children to behave in school, and most recognize how important discipline is to a successful education. In fact, for sixteen of the past seventeen years the public has identified discipline as the most serious problem facing its schools. Parents say that they know their children cannot get the most from education without fair and effective discipline, and research supports a definite correlation between good behavior and academic success.*

As a teacher, I find behavior problems the most frustrating part of education. One child bent on causing trouble can disrupt and take away educational time for the other thirty in the class. He can

---

* *What Works* (Washington, D.C.: U.S. Department of Education, 1986), p. 47.

and does put a damper on another student's willingness to ask questions or venture creative answers. Teachers spend time that they could really use for grading and lesson plans trying to develop strategies to get positive participation and involvement from those few in the class who are generally trying to disrupt it.

Certainly, discipline is an area in which parents and schools need to work together. Regretfully there are many stumbling blocks along the way in which egos and tempers interfere. Yet I firmly believe that if every parent were committed to working with the schools to improve discipline, public schools would be far more effective.

YOU'RE NOT THE ONE IN TROUBLE!

As an educator, I can absolutely assure you that you can deal far better with your child's behavior problems if you don't feel that you have failed as a parent because he has gotten in trouble. All kids, even the best behaved, occasionally strain at rules and push for independence by testing just what the limitations really are. Yet, as a parent, I can sympathize with the guilt most parents feel believing that somehow they have failed as a parent because their child has misbehaved. Unfortunately, these guilt feelings get in the way of an effective parent-teacher relationship to correct the child's behavior.

For example, not long ago a sixth-grade class gave a substitute teacher a terrible time. Particularly at fault were four students whose behavior was totally unacceptable. The principal called each of the child's parents and asked to meet with them. No doubt all of the parents were a little uneasy before their meeting, but the way each handled it was quite informative in seeing what makes discipline work or fail.

The principal met with the parents individually. He told them what kinds of things their child had done to the substitute, and that he hoped he and they could work together to improve the child's attitude. He felt it was particularly important because the sixth graders were role models for the younger kids in the school.

The first parent made his position clear immediately. "I handle Jimmy at home just fine. I don't call the school when I need to discipline him, and I don't believe the school should call me. Besides, at home Jimmy is respectful of everyone."

The subtle message here is that the parent isn't responsible for the child's misbehavior because the child doesn't misbehave at home. It alleviates the guilt the parent has been feeling, but it gives many negative messages the parent didn't intend. It tells the child that school and home are two separate things entirely, and the school is not the parent's concern. Students then jump to the conclusion that school doesn't really much matter at all, and they continue to push harder at the limitations school has set. The school can set penalties for misbehavior, but they don't mean much if the parents won't buy into them. That doesn't mean you should go along if you feel that the school is wrong; it just means that you should consider why you're upset and reacting the way you are before you say anything.

Josh's mother apologized. "He's so difficult to control. I don't think he means anything by his behavior. He's just so high-spirited. I don't blame you for being upset; I don't know how to handle him either."

Some principals say that they are hearing comments like this more and more frequently. It's a sad state; parents who are intimidated by their children. These kids already have it all figured out. They can do whatever they want because from an early age, they're used to getting away with it. Why should they listen to their parents? This lack of respect for authority figures carries over to the school, and the teacher finds herself being challenged on everything that the student doesn't feel like doing.

Tammi's father concluded that the school should get better substitutes. "I know my Tammi, and she hasn't had any trouble with her regular teachers at all. She never has done real well with substitutes. I think it's hard on all the kids to have the regular teacher gone."

Tammi's father may be right. Kids usually do like it better when their regular routine is not disrupted. Though that does not excuse

Tammi's behavior, Tammi may think it does because of her father's comments about the situation. In fact, if they are not careful, parents like Tammi's create an ongoing behavior problem. Nothing is ever the child's fault. There is always an extenuating circumstance and a reason to blame it on someone else. That means that poor behavior needs no correction or apology; instead, it simply means finding a scapegoat upon which to heap the blame. Teachers see a lot of this. If a child cheats on a test, he excuses it by saying that the test was too detailed. If a child gets cut from a team, he maintains it's only because the coach doesn't like him. If a child forgets to bring his books to school, he asserts that it's the teacher's fault for giving him homework that made him take the books home in the first place.

The bottom line is that kids must learn to take the consequences of their actions. You must instill in your child that it doesn't matter who else was bad; to you it only matters whether what he did was right or wrong.

That is exactly what Diane's mother did. She listened to the principal carefully and thanked him for taking the time to talk with her about the problem. "I don't think that Diane is a bad child, but I don't want this kind of thing to get out of hand. I'll certainly make it clear at home that her father and I expect her to respect substitute teachers, but I'd like to know what the school has planned."

The principal said that he was going to ask each child involved to serve an hour of after-school detention. "That's fine," said Diane's mother, "but would it be possible for Diane to interview some of the substitute teachers here first and spend her hour of detention writing about what it is like to be a substitute teacher?"

Diane's mother made it clear that she was working as a team with the school and didn't approve of the lack of respect her daughter gave the substitute; however, she also felt comfortable suggesting a way to make the punishment more relevant and valuable. The night after the assignment was completed, Diane admitted that she'd never really thought about substitute teachers as people before.

A high school coach said one of the saddest decisions he ever had to make was to bench a star pitcher because the boy was caught drinking. The rules stated that no athlete could use alcohol, and even though without this pitcher the coach knew that the team would lose the state title, he adhered to the rules. "Each kid had signed a contract at the beginning of the season about acceptable behavior, and he broke the contract. It was tough on the team, it was tough on me to lose him, but the toughest of all was having to defend myself in lengthy and involved conferences with the boy's parents. They were never really able to accept the fact that since the boy had knowingly broken a team rule with the consequences fully labeled ahead of time, he had to accept the responsibility of his actions. How else can we teach that important lesson?"

KEEP YOUR CHILD OUT OF TROUBLE

Of course, no child is a perfect angel, and it is unrealistic to assume that yours will grow up without ever having done a single thing wrong. However, we in education have noticed that there are some things you can do as a parent to minimize the possibility of your child getting into trouble.

- Know where your child is and with whom he is playing. Peer groups have tremendous influence on children. Given the right setting, your child is probably capable of doing things you would never have believed possible. Acceptance is a powerful reason for misbehavior, and it can often be avoided if you know your child's friends.

- Make certain that he knows your house is always open to his friends. There are several good reasons for this. First of all, it avoids having him associate with people because they are forbidden. Second, it allows you to see what his friends are like and to keep an eye on their activities. Finally, in the context of your own home, it gives your child a chance to see whether his friends fit in with your family's lifestyle and values. You cannot monitor your child's every move, but you can make home an inviting place. You cannot select every one of his friends, but you can keep a pulse on whether he's beginning to associate with a peer group that's headed for trouble.

- Keep your child involved in positive activities. A child with too much unsupervised time on his hands is one who is ripe for getting in trouble. It's hard if you're a full-time working parent to worry about extra activities; in fact, sometimes it seems difficult just to manage the required ones, yet the results are worth the effort. Check with your child's school to find out what kinds of alternatives are available to letting your child be a latchkey kid. Frequently, the YMCA, the YWCA, or other community facilities offer programs at a nominal cost. If there isn't anything you're satisfied with, try banding with other parents in a similar situation and forming some kind of after-school group for your children. Today it is estimated that almost five million children between five and thirteen are latchkey kids,* so you're certainly not alone in your needs. The time it takes you to help establish a community program will be well worth the peace of mind it gives.

- Encourage your child to take part in the extracurricular activities offered after school. They will help him feel more a part of the school and they will keep him out of other activities you'd rather he avoid. Don't depend on your child to find out what's available. One mother mentioned to me that it was a shame that schools no longer had clubs as they had when she was in school. "But they do," I said. "We must have at least fourteen. We have foreign language clubs, drama clubs, service clubs, sports pep clubs, etc."

The mother seemed quite surprised. "Why, my son said that there was nothing going on after school." I'm certain her son wasn't being deliberately deceitful. It's amazing how many kids walk

---

* *Kids with Keys . . . Parents with Jobs . . . Who's in Charge?* (National PTA pamphlet) p. 2.

around with blinders on and don't hear about anything which they or their friends are not immediately involved in. As a parent, you can check with the school or look through school yearbooks or guidelines to find out what's available, then encourage your child to join some of the activities.

Sometimes, however, your child resents and rejects all of your suggestions in which case you may need to become a little more inventive. That's what Myra found as she despairingly watched her fourteen-year-old daughter start to pal around with kids Myra really didn't like. She said, "As my daughter entered high school, many of her friends became more popular than she was and dropped her. I could see my daughter searching for a new peer group, and I didn't like the one she was finding. She and I were at each other's throats. She was feeling insecure, and therefore, she defensively rejected anything I suggested. Finally, I quit suggesting. I told the family it was about time I devoted some interest to some things I wanted to do, and I went to a church in our neighborhood and offered to help sponsor the youth group there. The next meeting was at our house. I didn't tell my daughter that she had to come or had to be involved, but the kids were all there; they were all having fun, and soon she was too. I think she knew those other kids weren't right. I don't think she even liked them. I just think she was afraid to risk being left out again."

- Focus on the positive that your child accomplishes. We all like to hear compliments. Don't simply accept the good things your child does as what he should be doing. The parent who mentions, "Look at all these comments on your papers saying you're showing good effort. I'm so proud of you," is likely to have a child who continues to try even if he doesn't always get things perfect. Be the parent who first comments on the eight right instead of the two that are wrong.

- Talk with your child about the need for discipline. If he comments to you that he doesn't like having to raise his hand, ask him to imagine his classroom if no one ever raised his hand before speaking. Make sure he understands the basis for having rules in a classroom and at home.

WHEN YOUR CHILD DOES GET INTO DIFFICULTY

Very few (if any) children go all the way through school without ever having the need to be disciplined. How will you handle it when your child brings home the note from the principal or the unsatisfactory in behavior or some other indication of a halo that's slipped? Your actions and your attitudes can make a big difference in whether the infractions disappear or get worse.

1. Talk about the matter with your child but try not to get angry. That can easily sabotage you before you ever begin, as this example shows. A mother looks at her child's report card and sees an unsatisfactory in citizenship. "Why did you get this?" she asks.

"I have no idea," he says.

"You have no idea?" repeats the parent skeptically. "What do you mean you have no idea?"

"Well, I guess my teacher just had to give so many of them, and I got one."

By this time the parent is furious. "That's the stupidest thing I've ever heard of. When I ask you a question, you answer it. She probably gave you a U because you're an idiot! Only an idiot would have no idea what he did wrong."

Obviously, this conversation has not gotten off to a good start. Soon the parent will feel so badly about calling her son an idiot that she will want to forget the entire conversation without ever having gotten to the root of the problem.

Kids are aware of this gambit. In fact, some of them use it regularly. They advise their friends to try to make their folks really angry about something else, saying that if they can provoke their parents enough, the original issue can be totally avoided.

2. Talk with your child about why he did what he did. What did he gain from his actions? Listen to his answers, but be careful at this point, for this can easily be a booby-trapped situation and Brad's mother fell right into it. She was quite concerned when Brad's teacher called to say that the second-grader was ripping up other students' papers. This was becoming a real problem. She explained that she'd talked to Brad; she'd even made him stay in during recess and recopy one of the papers he'd torn up, but his behavior wasn't improving. The teacher asked for Brad's mother's reinforcement that such behavior had to cease. Brad's mother said that she was glad the teacher had called, and she'd talk to Brad.

Brad's mother began by asking why he'd ripped up other kids' papers and he replied with every child's favorite answer, "I don't know." His mother persisted in saying that there must be a reason. Brad answered, "I just feel like doing that sometimes." Brad's mother asked again, "But why do you feel like doing that?" The conversation continued. Brad's mother was determined to get to the psychological bottom of this issue before she punished him. Meanwhile, Brad continued ripping up other kids' papers whenever he felt like it.

While it's definitely important to communicate with your children and to find out what motivates them, it's also important to remember that kids can be very manipulative. When a child's behavior is clearly unacceptable, you as his parent must not hesitate in affirming that the behavior has to be stopped immediately.

3. Talk about the consequences of your child's negative actions. How can the harm he's created be repaid? What are the school's rules about such behavior? Most schools have clearly spelled out rules and penalties for breaking those rules. Help your child to see that he made the decision to break the rules; therefore, he will have to accept the punishment. Refuse to let yourself be made to feel guilty because your child says you're mean or the school is mean. You didn't stand over him making him cheat from the paper on the desk ahead of his. He decided to do so; therefore, he will have to accept the consequences of that decision.

Letting kids accept the consequences of their behavior is sometimes harder on the parents than the children. One father came in to see me about two months ago, trying to get me to change his daughter's poor grade. "You see," he said sadly, "I promised her a brand-new car for her sixteenth birthday if she got a C average, but unless you change her English grade, she won't make it." More to himself than to me he said, "I'd really like to give her that car. When I was sixteen, I wanted a car more than anything in the world, but my folks couldn't afford it. Now I can afford the best for my daughter, and damn it, I want to be able to give it to her."

4. Be consistent in your rules, expectations, and punishments. The end to the above story is a perfect example of why this is important. I did not change the girl's grade, but two weeks later, I saw her driving her new car from school. Her father had sworn that unless she got the C average, there'd be no car, but when she failed to complete the responsibility, he changed the rules. I wonder what will happen the next time he sets down conditions.

An elementary school principal gives another example. "I had a parent in my office who agreed that what her child did was wrong and to reinforce that, she said that she would ground the child from watching television after school for two weeks. Three days later, the child was at school discussing all the after-school television programs with his friends. How did this happen? The parent worked until six at night, leaving the child home alone with no one to monitor the after-school punishment that was given."

It's so important that parents be consistent by giving punishments which they can uphold. Otherwise, what meaning has the punishment?

5. Be realistic in your punishments. A fifth-grade teacher contacted a parent about the fact that her child was not doing any of his spelling homework, and would the parent mind if he was kept after school for a few minutes each day to do some extra spelling work. "I'll do better than that," exclaimed the angry parent. "I'll make him copy the dictionary." This, of course, turned out to be an impossible punishment. The parent had to back down, and so the punishment had little meaning. Besides, it had nothing to do with learning the spelling words presented in class.

6. If the teacher and your child have set up a plan of discipline, be supportive in holding your child accountable for that plan. Again, the reason here is that the child needs to see the school and home working together, and the child needs to see that the parent supports his taking the consequences of his actions.

7. After the initial discovery and discussion, talk with your child about what he can change to ensure that the discipline problem doesn't happen again. If he keeps getting in trouble for talking, maybe he should ask to be moved to a seat that isn't near his best friend. If he's accumulating too many tardies, maybe you and he should figure out a morning schedule that will allow him more time. In other words, work with your child to allow him to discover ways that he can prevent the same discipline problem from resurfacing.

These steps will help to solve the immediate discipline problem, but more important, they will help the child to become a responsible person and see that there is an accepted standard of behavior which is shared by school and home alike.

Many kids today have an attitude of "I don't care" that is difficult for older people to understand. Perhaps it is because this generation of children has never had to live through a war or a depression; many of them simply expect that things will come to them and will work out, regardless of what they do or don't do. Whatever the reason, student apathy creates a host of academic and discipline problems.

One of the best teachers I know offered any student who was failing her class a chance to pass if the student would sign up for after-school help twice a week. Fewer than three percent of the eligible students took her up on her offer, and those who did come in told her to hurry. They only had ten minutes or they'd be home too late to watch reruns of *Little House on the Prairie.*

How can you circumvent your child's being in such a position? Let your child know from the beginning of his schooling that education is important, that doing his best is expected, and that while you will provide help as needed, failure will not be lightly accepted. It's too late to suddenly start espousing all this when the child is in high school; it must begin when he is first starting school.

Over and over again, educators stress two things for success in school—good attendance and stick-to-it-iveness. As one principal said, "I've been around for a long time, and I've come to the conclusion that IQ doesn't matter nearly as much as PQ (perseverance quotient). Success doesn't have to be a straight A student. Success is the student who is at school every day learning as much as he possibly can."

WHAT IF THE SCHOOL IS WRONG?

If you feel that your child has been accused or punished unfairly, by all means, look into it. You owe it to yourself and your child. However, remember that there are always two sides to every story, and you need to make appointments with the school to find out its side before you charge like a raging bull. If you are not pleased with the answers you get, you can take further action. You can appeal the situation through the principal to the superintendent and then to the school board. If you are still unhappy, you may have legal recourse.

Many of your rights as a parent are designated by the laws of your state. However, here is a general look at those rights as found in "Parents Rights Card."*

---

* National Committee for Citizens in Education, 1985.

1. Student Discipline. You have the right to take legal action against a school official who uses "excessive or unreasonable physical" force to discipline your child. You have the right to appeal the suspension of your child from school in Washington, D.C. and all states except Kansas, Utah, and Wisconsin.

2. School Policies. You have the right to look at all official school policies and to examine the school budget. You also have the right to look at all of your child's school records and to challenge any record that you feel is unfair or untrue. School officials must respond to your challenge within a reasonable period of time; if you're not pleased with their response, you may request a hearing.

3. Student Search. School officials must have reasonable suspicion to believe that a school rule or law has been violated before searching your child. The way the search is conducted must be reasonably related to its objective and circumstances. If you feel that the search was unreasonable, you can appeal any action, policy, or decision permitting it.

4. Book Banning. You can challenge the removal of books from the school library based on school officials' personal dislike of the books.

You can obtain a Parents Rights Card by writing to the National Committee for Citizens in Education, 10840 Little Patuxent Parkway, Suite 301, Columbia MD 21044-2396. It lists twenty-three rights that you may have as a parent of a child in public schools, and details in which states the rights exist. The cost is twenty-five cents.

While knowing your rights is certainly important in letting you protect your child from unfair treatment or abuse by educators, it's important to use them wisely. Threats of suits have allowed some troublemakers to mock the teacher's authority and disrupt class. Be careful that an overstated concern for principle doesn't undermine your child's education.

For example, recently a nine-year-old boy called his teacher a

F---ing B----. Appalled, his teacher demanded that he write that he was sorry one hundred times. The parent appealed the ruling to the principal. "He didn't write anything wrong, he said something wrong. The punishment doesn't fit the crime." The principal upheld the punishment. The parent took this case all the way through the school system. She argued, "I'm not saying that he should speak that way, only that it isn't fair to make him write an apology out. It's a matter of principle. I'll be glad to support his saying he's sorry one hundred times; I just won't make him write it."

Meanwhile, the child was strutting around school as if he had accomplished a real coup. More than a week had passed since his outburst in front of the class, and he still hadn't completed the punishment, because his parents were involved in the due process of protesting it. The message to the other children seemed to be that Jason was a kind of an "outlaw-hero" who could do anything he wanted in class. They, too, thought it would be interesting to try to break the rules, and discipline became a major problem in the classroom.

It's not easy to discipline effectively, but it's certainly worth the effort to try. As I must discipline my own children, I try to remember the words of Clifford K. Madsen and Charles H. Madsen, Jr., from *Parents/Children/Discipline, A Positive Approach* (Boston: Allyn and Bacon, 1972, pp. 192–3). They said, "The reason we discipline is to provide each child with behaviors necessary for individual productivity and happiness." And though it's difficult to discipline at times, what parent wouldn't want to ultimately help his child be productive and happy?

EIGHT

SCHOOL
RESOURCE
PEOPLE

Suspecting a learning problem, Bobby's concerned parents decided to take him to a psychologist for tests. The cost of the tests was an unplanned expense on an already tight budget, but there was no question in his parents' minds that it was worth the money. After all, Bobby seemed to be struggling and what could possibly be more important than helping their child find success in school? The family would have to do without something else that month, but Bobby would be tested.

Though his parents' intentions were admirable and their decision to seek help wise, the strain on their pocketbook simply wasn't necessary. The tests they paid a private psychologist over two hundred dollars to administer and interpret were available to Bobby at no charge through his school district's psychologist. So why didn't these concerned parents simply go to the district in the first place? The answer was sad but quite simple. They had no idea such a service was even available. In fact, they didn't find out until they requested a conference with Bobby's teacher to share the results of the tests. "I'm pleased to know these things," said his teacher, "but I am a little curious. Is there any particular reason you didn't want to have these tests done at school?"

Bobby's father shrugged helplessly. "Why didn't you suggest it to us? We didn't realize we could."

"Actually, I've been thinking about calling you to talk about having Bobby tested. I decided I'd observe him a little longer first, but I'd have been quite comfortable in recommending that he be tested if I'd known you and I had the same concerns."

Bobby's case is not extraordinary. It's easy for kids on the cusp to be overlooked when it comes to special resources. The child who is a genius, the child who cannot read, or the one who is destroying the classroom is likely to get plenty of notice and special placement. The child who is marginal may wait a long time unless he has an alert parent who knows what the system has to offer.

Unfortunately, there are not too many parents in this category. Most parents make an effort to know who their child's teachers are, but beyond that, they're fuzzy on who does what in a school and how those jobs affect their child. A Gallup Poll on public awareness of local schools found that fewer than half the respondents could even name the principals of either their neighborhood elementary or high school.

The responsibility and titles of school resource people vary from school to school and certainly from state to state, so the purpose of this chapter is intended to give you a broad overview of what's available as well as what these people can and can't do for your child.

THE PRINCIPAL

Of course you know that your child's school has one, but what should you expect from him or her?

The principal is a key resource person to answer questions about the operation of the school or the programs within it. She is the single most important person in setting the school climate and rules. Almost every school cited by the Department of Education as outstanding stressed the leadership, dedication, and communication abilities of its principal.

The principal is the individual who must prepare the school budget, act as an instructional leader for the staff, serve as a liaison between the district office and the school, and evaluate the teachers and classified employees on her staff.

Obviously that keeps her a very busy person, but you should never make the mistake of thinking that means she is too busy for you, the parent of a child in her school. *It is her job to be accessible* and to meet with parents who want to see her. Yet some parents fail to take advantage of her availability. You're certainly not alone if a visit to the principal still conjures up some butterflies in your stomach, but remember, you're both adults now on equal footing, and she may be a valuable aid to your child.

There are many examples of interference by a principal making a significant difference in a child's education. One mother of a third-grade boy who had always done well in school realized that her son was beginning to refuse to do his homework or to discuss school. The mother contacted the principal (although this author still believes that she should have started with the teacher and gone to the principal if dissatisfied). Though the mother felt fairly certain that the math teacher was the root of the problem, she did not attack the teacher in her presentation to the principal. She simply said that her son's problem seemed to be centered in math, and that she needed to find a way to keep him motivated and interested in completing his schoolwork. "He seems to have gotten into an argument with the teacher over work he says he turned in, and she says he didn't. I don't know if he turned it in, but I did see him do the work. Also, though he may not be the one to judge, he has been complaining for some time that the math teacher gives a great deal of homework. What can you do to help me get my child back on target?"

The principal was grateful for the mother's approach because it had been centered on the child and had been done in a positive manner which made it much easier for the principal to be helpful. "Why don't we try this?" the principal replied. "Let's set up an assignment sheet. I'll ask the teachers to write each day's assignments on the sheet; that way you can see exactly what your child has as homework. You initial the sheet when you've seen the completed assignment, and I'll ask the teacher to make a check mark the day she receives it from your son. That way you can monitor things on a constant basis. I suggest that for each week he gets everything completed, you provide him with a special reward, perhaps a game with you, or going out for an ice-cream cone. I think your support will mean a great deal to your son. Meanwhile, I'll look into some things here at school, and please do get back to me and let me know how things are working out."

Later the principal confided that this assignment sheet would serve a number of other functions. It would give her a perfect opportunity to see whether there was some basis for concern over the length of the math assignments, and it would also give the teacher a chance to see in black and white what her assignments were like in comparison to the other teachers during the school day.

In fact, the math teacher noticed that her assignments were longer than anyone else's and that combined with reading and language, the requirements were over the district's recommended homework guidelines. The principal, in reviewing the assignment sheets, was able to suggest certain types of things that could easily be dropped without lessening learning, and the child, with his parent's guidance, realized that he shouldn't simply quit whenever he got into a situation he felt unfair.

Not all conferences produce such positive results. Just the other day, a parent-principal conference went like this. "My son is totally turned off school. His English teacher is boring him to death. Now my tax dollars support this place, and I'm certainly not getting my money's worth if my child hates school. In fact, I don't think most kids like school today; when I was growing up, things were different."

You can just about guess what tone the conference took on. The principal became rather defensive, the parent became more assertive, and the conversation ended up focusing on philosophical points of what American education should or should not have to do. The child's problem got lost along the way.

There are some things that a principal cannot do for you, and understanding them will help you to have a beneficial relationship with your child's school. For example, one principal said, "The other day a very agitated mother came into the school. She wanted me to get rid of the science teacher. She maintained that not only was her son learning nothing, but neither was any other child who'd ever had him."

The principal sighed deeply. "This is a very vague kind of complaint. Maybe the child is learning, maybe he isn't; and if he isn't, why not? I asked the woman if she'd be willing to write something specific that I could keep on file, but she got angry, saying she didn't come to get a runaround, and she certainly didn't come to do my job for me. Now, off the record, I don't think this teacher is all that great myself, but that doesn't mean I can walk into her room and fire her. Unless she practically kills someone in the classroom, I've got to get a pile of documentation ten inches thick before I can get rid of her."

Most school districts in the country have a due-process system which demands specific documentation and a hearing before a teacher can be fired from her job. If you're trying to get rid of a poor teacher, this is a good point to remember. Try to find out what sort of information you need to produce or gather to help in the ouster of such a teacher.

Principals often get requests to change the time of the school day's beginning, to add a program to the curriculum, to change a bus route, to make kindergarten a full day, but there is little they can do to implement any of those things because all require funds or authority that principals simply do not have. One principal confided, "I think some parents still see me as the large authority figure they remembered as students, but really my direct powers are limited in many ways." Of course that doesn't mean you must give up on things beyond the principal's jurisdiction; in fact she may be an excellent resource person for you to contact in finding out just whom to get in touch with about making the desired change and how to go about it.

THE SCHOOL SECRETARY

Many people who've been involved in education for a while laughingly say that the school secretary is the best source of immediate information in the entire school. There is some validity to that. After all, from her vantage point, she sees a great deal of everything that goes on. What can she do for you?

In many cases, she's been given the task of screening the principal's calls. Some parents take this as a direct snub. "I hate the inference," says one mother, "that someone is checking to see if I'm important enough to talk to the principal. It's intimidating."

However, school secretaries say that the intent is not to intimidate at all. Consider that the principal may get seven phone calls during the time that he is in conference with a parent. Yet most of those callers may actually only want information which the secretary has at her fingertips. She doesn't have to interrupt the principal, nor does the caller have to wait for a return call for answers. One secretary says, "By screening calls, I'm not trying to pry at all, I'm just trying to get each parent prompt, accurate information as fast as possible."

If you need to speak to the principal, and you don't wish to share the subject matter with the school secretary, that is certainly your right; when she says, "What is this in reference to?" you have only to reply that you'd prefer to give the details to the principal when you speak with him. However, don't complicate your life unnecessarily. I remember the mother who called for an appointment with the principal, waited for him to return her call, and when she finally spoke to him and asked for an appointment, he replied, "I'd be more than happy to meet with you. Let me just put on my secretary and she'll make the appointment when it's convenient for you."

Frequently in a large high school she is a ready source of such information as the last date for boys' physicals for baseball eligibility, which day the following week is a half-day schedule, or what teacher might be most interested in contacting a dynamic speaker who is willing to talk to students. The school secretary in a large high school usually does not handle any attendance matters; those are the function of an attendance secretary who is also available to you to answer questions.

In a smaller elementary school, the school secretary is a tremendous source of networked information. I've seen people call the school secretary to leave their names as after-school babysitters, and working mothers call her to ask if she knows of anyone close to school who babysits. She frequently serves as a repository for forgotten lunches, jackets, and backpacks that parents drop off for their children to collect.

So while the school secretary can help you get to the right person to handle a problem or serve as part of an informal network, there are some things she'd like parents to understand.

Don't vent your anger on her. Of course you're upset because your child has just come home in tears. However, calling the school secretary to complain doesn't solve a thing.

Don't put her in the middle of a disagreement you are having with another staff member. One secretary says, "I'm always amazed at the number of parents who come to me and want me to bolster their case against a teacher by sharing any bad things I know. That would be unethical."

Don't assume that the secretary is your child's extra mother at school. Occasionally she can relay a message to your child, hang on to a lunch you've delivered, etc., but there are some parents who consider these things her primary job, and it isn't.

THE SCHOOL NURSE

Mrs. Landing was upset when she heard about the experience her seventh-grade daughter had had with the school nurse that day. The girl had requested two aspirin, explaining, "I get these awful headaches every once in a while and aspirin always helps."

But in spite of the child's logical explanation, the nurse refused the request. "You can either lie down in here for an hour, go back to class, or I can call your mother to take you home. I cannot give you two aspirin."

The child tried lying down for an hour, but it didn't help much. She didn't want to call her mother to leave work and pick her up, and besides, she really wanted to stay at school and take a big test for which she'd studied hard, so she suffered through the day. By the time she got home, she felt sick to her stomach from the pain throbbing in her head. Her agitated mother said, "There was no reason for my child to be in pain when the nurse could have ended it with two little aspirin!"

According to many school nurses this is an ongoing problem. In most schools, the nurse is not allowed to give medication without the parent's written request, and if prescription it cannot be given without a physician's written order. This may seem overly restrictive, but it is done for your child's own protection.

So what can the school nurse do for your child? It will vary depending on the nurse's philosophy and expertise and the school's policy and budget. Financial considerations have left a number of schools with aides as nurses instead of RN's. The less experience and expertise a nurse or "acting" nurse has, the fewer services she is going to feel comfortable in offering your child. However, you can expect that she'll treat minor cuts and attend your child in an emergency until medical experts arrive.

The school nurse will keep track of the medication that is supposed to be administered to your child and give it as prescribed. If you have any concerns about this, you shouldn't hesitate to see the nurse. One mother had to leave a Maxi-Mist air compressor/nebulizer at school for her daughter's asthma condition. She said, "When I dropped off the machine and medication to go in it, I wanted to say something to the nurse about how to use it. I didn't want my daughter trying to explain it while gasping for breath, but then I hesitated because I figured she was the nurse and I'd be insulting her. Then at the last minute, I gathered up my nerve and asked her if she'd like me to show her how it worked. The nurse said she'd be glad to have the demonstration since she hadn't used a machine like this one in years. Yet I think if I hadn't asked, she'd have muddled through it because she was embarrassed to say anything to me."

If your child must have restricted physical education, it is likely that it will be the nurse's job to inform the coach. It is the nurse who apprises all other school personnel about the nature of a child's medical problems. Basically it comes down to the fact that she's the primary contact between your child's doctor and the school. Parents who withhold health information from her because they feel it's private can actually make a health situation more difficult for their child. Telling the nurse your child has epilepsy will not in any way lessen him in her eyes, but it will be important for her to know if he has an episode.

The nurse is frequently the one in charge of vision and hearing screening programs (and usually welcomes parent assistance in both). Some conduct first-aid classes and family and sex education classes in addition to their other duties.

A great deal of the nurse's time is spent on paperwork. Her duties include keeping the health records on each child in the school and coordinating and keeping immunization records. In addition, many nurses have been given responsibilities in attendance and record-keeping procedures.

You should find out if your school has a full-time nurse, and if not, who is responsible for handling injuries and illness. If your child may need medication for a sporadic problem, you should make certain you have the proper medication with the proper documentation available for him at the school.

If your child has been absent because of a prolonged illness, talk to the nurse when he's ready to return to school. Make sure you use this opportunity to spell out any of your concerns or the potential problems you feel he might face. The school nurse can be a great help, as the following story shows.

Bill had just finished grammar school and although all his classmates were excited about going on to high school, Bill dreaded the thought. A victim of spina bifida, he had to wear diapers, and he couldn't imagine how he'd handle having to change them in the high school restrooms. A visit between the nurse and his mother resulted in Bill's being assured of a private place to change and passes to excuse tardies without having to give any reason that would violate his wish to keep his condition confidential from teachers and fellow students.

THE LIBRARIAN

Forget your memories of the school librarian as a stern-faced old lady who was always telling you to be quiet. In today's schools, the library is often the hub of the school. Because the library is often open extended hours before and after school, the librarian can become a real friend to your child. Just how much of a friend can be illustrated by an incident that occurred recently at the high school in which I teach. A sixteen-year-old boy, thrilled to finally begin behind-the-wheel driving in his driver's education class, absent-mindedly put his books on top of the car while he talked to a friend. He then waved good-bye to the friend, having forgotten all about the books, and got in the car, backed up, and drove over the books as they fell from the roof. Horrified, he leaped from the car, looked at the remnants of his books and went straight to the school librarian. "I'm going to get killed," he said. "Mrs. Dunn, is there anything you can do to help me?"

The librarian helped him rebind one book and then gave him the materials to rebind the rest. He still owed a fine on the books, but it wasn't much, and the books were usable for the rest of the year. Later he told the librarian that he might use his newfound book-binding skill for a class project in English.

If your school is fortunate enough to have a full-time professional librarian, you should have a valuable resource for helping your children appreciate reading. Again the role varies from school to school, and some school districts cannot afford a librarian at all.

Generally, in the primary grades most librarians work quite hard to help your children get interested in books. They sponsor reading contests with prizes for children who read the most books; they read aloud from some of the books they think children would enjoy; they decide what books to order for the library; and they try to make the atmosphere there seem warm and inviting enough to encourage children to stop in and explore. You might consider talking with your school librarian to see what books she'd suggest for your child's summer reading.

On the high school level, the librarian's focus is more on helping teens learn to be successful in using resource and research material so that the student can write the papers required of him in high school and college. One librarian explains, "Parents and students often don't quite understand our purpose. It is to help children learn to be self-sufficient in the library. Not too long ago, a boy came to me and asked me to give him information on ozone pollution. He said he had to do a term paper on it, and could I hurry and get him the material because his mother was waiting in the car. What neither he nor she understood was that I could have just given him some information, and the next time he had a report to do, he'd still have had no idea how to find the information for himself. Though it takes longer, I'd be doing less than my job if I didn't show him sources and how to use them and then let him find the actual material himself."

Many librarians must also deal with questions of censorship. Most feel that it is much better for a parent to be aware of what his children are reading and to discuss it with them within the limits of the family values than to summarily try to have books of literary merit pulled from the shelves.

Librarians can be a great help in turning your children on to reading and a valuable resource in presenting ways to use source and research material. However, they ask that you help them to help your child by doing the following:

- Encourage your child to return books on time. At the end of the year in one elementary school, a boy had forty-eight unreturned books. Calls to his house gained the sheepish admission from his mother that she'd noticed a lot of books around, and she'd try to get him to return them, but at least it was great that he liked to read.

  Kids need parental reinforcement to feel a sense of responsibility and pride in being able to borrow and return material when it is due.

- Love reading at home. "Whatever we do in school," admits one librarian, "can't hold a candle to the parent who frequently reads to his child and who lets that child see that he enjoys and reads often himself."

● Find out what your child's assignments are and when they are due. Encourage him to go to the library as soon as possible. Librarians say, "We can't begin to give your child the help he deserves if he's left himself only one night to get the whole project done." They talk about staying late after school and keeping the library open to accommodate last-minute students, but they say that children's procrastination leaves everyone feeling frustrated.

THE SCHOOL PSYCHOLOGIST

While school districts have psychologists, most individual schools do not have full-time psychologists on site. Therefore, some parents fail to realize that a psychologist is available to them, and if they do find out, they frequently don't understand what the psychologist can and cannot do for their child.

Not uncommon are the feelings of initial anger that Mandy's mother expressed when she said. "That dumb school. The psychologist there says that my Mandy needs special counseling, so I bite my lip and say okay, then go ahead and start seeing her. Then the psychologist says no, she doesn't do that sort of thing, but she can suggest people who do. So I ask her if those people are psychologists and she says that some of them are. Now I ask you, does that make sense?"

Though at first glance it may not seem to make much sense at all, there is an easy explanation. A clinical psychologist is an individual who primarily works in individual or group counseling, and she is quite different from a school psychologist who is there primarily to evaluate your child in terms of discovering why he is or is not achieving and whether the school can be the best agency to help him. The school psychologist's workload in this area precludes any real time for individual counseling sessions. Furthermore, she would not be there over critical times during holidays or summer vacation.

To get a better idea of what she does do, let's follow a school psychologist through one case. Jimmy is referred by two of his teachers who are concerned about the way he is progressing. His parents are called to ask if they will approve his being tested and they consent. The case is then turned over to the school psychologist. From the time she first begins Jimmy's case until the conference about him takes place, the psychologist spends about eight hours determining how to help him. Before she ever meets him, she observes him in the classroom. Later, she introduces herself and talks with him about the tests he is going to take. She's upbeat and positive so that the test experience will not be threatening. Based on the information she has gotten from his teachers and what she has seen so far, she decides to give him an individual achievement test to get a better picture of his skill in reading, written expression, and/or math, and an individual IQ test to show his ability to learn. Since behavior has not really been a problem, she will skip giving him personality tests. To keep him from missing too much class time and to make certain that he is fresh and able to do his best, she'll test him for a short period over two days.

The tests finished, Jimmy goes back to class, and the psychologist begins to carefully compile the information she has learned and to evaluate what would best help him. Once she has completed this task, she requests a multidisciplinary conference. This is very important, because contrary to what some parents initially think, she does not make the final decision on their child. It is a group process, and parents are very much encouraged to be part of it. At Jimmy's conference, his classroom teacher talks about his homework and class participation. His parents are asked how he functions at home, and to talk about his developmental history academically and socially. Then the psychologist explains and interprets the tests she's administered and reminds the parents of their rights under the laws concerning special education. A special-education teacher at Jimmy's school attends the meeting and explains how she thinks she can help the boy in her program. After everyone's input, the psychologist explains the alternatives available to Jimmy and his parents. They may choose to do nothing, to have Jimmy tutored privately, or to put him in the thrice-a-week special-education class for which he has qualified. Though his parents have entered the meeting feeling quite apprehensive, they have forced themselves to put aside their fears and ask questions until they feel certain they understand everything that's being said. They leave with a clearer understanding of why their child is having trouble in school and hope that the plan they have helped devise for him will help him to find success instead of the frustration he has been feeling.

Of course, the exact procedure the school psychologist uses will vary somewhat from school to school, but this example gives you an idea of what you might expect. As a parent, if you are to maximize your use of the school psychologist, keep these things in mind. Normally, a child is tested after being referred by several teachers; however, you can certainly request and keep requesting that your child be tested. You don't have to wait for a teacher to recommend him for testing. In fact, you may catch problems that a teacher with limited time and thirty kids a day misses.

Do realize that you have the right to ask for testing from a public-school psychologist *even* if your child is attending a private school. Call your public school district for details.

Do provide all the information that the psychologist asks you for in the testing process. It is not abnormal for her to ask for health and developmental history as well as information about cultural background. Please be as complete as possible in answering all questions about home life. "No one is prying," asserts one school psychologist, "but often the information is crucial in helping us make the right diagnosis."

As explained previously, don't expect to see a school psychologist on a regular basis, and don't expect follow-up of your child's progress daily or weekly.

Do consult her as a source for recommending a clinical psychologist or counselor for your child. Part of her job is to communicate with community mental-health facilities, special schools, psychiatrists, psychologists, and other resources offering services to your child. You do not have to have had a child tested by her nor must he be in the school special-education department for you to call asking for recommendations for community resources.

SPECIAL-EDUCATION RESOURCES

Nine-year-old Jenny reports to a learning-disabled class three times a week where the teacher works with her on math. At last, the numbers that floated around her for so long seem to be making some sense.

Fourteen-year-old Eileen has been blind since birth and her eighth-grade graduation with honors could not have been possible without the visually handicapped resource program that taught her how to maneuver the school grounds, how to read and write in Braille, and how to use her own Brailler.

Ten-year-old Ben meets with a hearing resource teacher every day to go over what he's doing in his regular classroom. He's of normal intelligence, but his hearing loss means that he misses much of the teacher's directions and explanations. The extra chance to make sure he understands the information has enabled him to function well in his regular classroom.

There are many different types of special-education teachers. Their purpose is to help your child succeed in the least restrictive environment possible. Programs range from self-contained classrooms in which the special-education student spends his entire day to resource teachers with whom the student checks in once or twice a week. There are programs for physically, emotionally, and mentally handicapped children. Programs for the gifted and talented also fall under the special-education category. Each child in a special-education program must have an Individual Educational Plan filled out for him which will include information about the goals designed for him to achieve as well as what type of services will be offered to achieve those goals. Parents must be shown these plans and they have the right to refuse to sign them or to suggest some changes be made in them.

The special-education teacher is able to help your child for several reasons. First and most importantly, she has special training in the particular area in which your child needs help. Secondly, she has a smaller group to work with and chances are your child will feel more comfortable in asking her questions. Finally, as a resource teacher, she will work with the regular teacher to suggest methods and plans to make the material clearer to your child if he is having trouble understanding it. In the case of the gifted, the resource teacher may suggest or design supplementary projects that will help keep the child interested and challenged.

HOMEBOUND TEACHER

Parents who might otherwise never come in contact with special education may find a need for the homebound teacher.

Such was the case with Joshua, a handsome sixteen-year-old boy who was doing well in school until he got involved with drugs. His parents got him into a hospital drug-rehabilitation program which was having a positive effect, but they worried that the amount of time he was missing at school would mean that he'd get so far behind, he'd have to repeat a year. To their vast relief, they found that the school district enrolled him in its homebound program, and when he was pronounced well enough by the hospital to go back to school, he was academically current and able to graduate with his class.

Seventeen-year-old Linda was in a car accident and hit her head on the windshield. It left her partially paralyzed and functioning on a first-grade level. The district's homebound teacher began working with her as soon as the doctor would allow, beginning with comic strips and working to show her how to sequence. When Linda was able to function in school again, the homebound teacher was part of the team that evaluated Linda's progress and found the best place for her to continue to achieve.

If your child must miss a lengthy period of school, it does not mean that he'll be left forever behind all of his friends. Many school districts have an active homebound program, and usually the only requirement is a doctor's letter saying that your child will be unable to attend school for a prolonged period of time. The homebound teacher will work with the child on a one-to-one basis allowing him to keep up with the schoolwork being done in his classroom and ensuring a smooth return if he makes it back before the end of the school year. However, parents are very important in making the homebound program successful for their child. The homebound teacher is only there for a very limited amount of time, and further direction must come from the parent. While the homebound teacher is at the child's home, it is up to the parent to make certain that distracting noises are controlled and that the child has no other responsibilities. After the teacher leaves, the parents should help to make certain that the child has his work ready and organized for the next teacher visit.

COUNSELORS

Some elementary schools have counselors, but they seem to be the exception rather than the rule, so I'll discuss the role of counselors primarily in terms of the junior high and high school. All of the counselors to whom I spoke work with ratios of one counselor to three or four hundred students. This makes truly knowing and working with the child almost impossible. Counselors seem mired in paperwork, and if your child does need clinical counseling, you may want to consider outside sources. However, dealing with an upset student over a confrontation with a teacher, a poor grade on a test, etc. are things they do every day, and frequently, an objective ear at a crucial moment is all the student needs.

Though counselors do talk with students about many things, their primary goal is to help students establish high goals in school and then devise a class program that will enable them to achieve those goals.

School counselors are a link between the parent and the teacher. If a parent is concerned about his child's general performance or attitude, he may wish to contact the counselor and let the counselor talk with each of the child's five to seven teachers. The counselor will then report back to the parent as to what general tendencies the teachers have noted.

Counselors keep track of a student's academic progress in school. They help the child decide what classes to take during high school and how to prepare academically for college or a career. You should feel free to contact your child's counselor if you have questions about the classes he is taking. In addition, the counselor is often a good source for scholarship information.

As schools have put increased importance on attendance, many counselors are being given the job of keeping parents informed of excessive absences and reminding parent and child of the possible consequences of too many absences.

Because much of their work involves both the child and the parent, they have several suggestions.

- If your child is transferring schools, make sure that he has his records to bring to the new school. One counselor said fewer than 5 percent of the new enrollees bring records from their old school. "I'm not sure parents realize what a problem this is. We go ahead and put the child in his classes based on what he and his parents say, then eventually, when we finally do get the records, we find out about classes he thought he took that he really didn't or vice versa. Often it means making changes and having to have a student adjust to new situations all over again."

- Don't make your child drop all his outside school interests if his grades drop. Counselors report seeing kids who used to love being at school find other far less desirable activities and places when the parent has taken away all sports, drama, etc. "Make him put in one hour of study for every hour he spends at football practice or something, but don't just say you're grounded from any more sports," suggests counselor Alan Osbon.

- Listen to your child carefully and reassure him that he can talk to you. Several counselors mentioned that students come to them with problems hoping that the counselor's solution will be to call their parents because the kids don't know how to approach the parent with the problem themselves.

Some schools are assigning special counselors to work on substance-abuse prevention; however, many others simply feel that the counselors are already too overburdened to take on any more work. Don't assume that such counseling is occurring at your child's school. Check it out for yourself.

UP THE LADDER

If you are unhappy with the response you've gotten to a concern that you have, you can always go up the ladder to the district office. However, if it is a school problem, begin at the school level. A quick survey of district administrators shows that if you decide you'll just start at the top and go to the superintendent, chances are he'll politely listen to you and then suggest you talk to an individual at your school and get back to him if that doesn't settle the problem.

However, suppose you were displeased with the way a teacher handled a discipline problem and you'd gone to the principal who simply told you that he always backed his teachers' discipline procedures. That doesn't have to be the end of the situation. You can call the school-district office and say, "I'd like to know to whom the principal reports, and then I'd like to speak with that person." In some districts that may be the superintendent; in some it may be an assistant superintendent. There is no need to divulge the details of your problem to the person who initially answers the phone.

Chances are that you will be connected to the individual's secretary. There is still no need to go into the details of the problem with her. Either ask the secretary about a time to set up a phone appointment with the person or better yet, set up a time for a personal appointment.

When you arrive, remember to stick to the rules of good conferencing. Don't waste time name-calling or trying to get the principal in trouble. Do bring notes if necessary to keep everything clear in your mind, but be ready to objectively present what happened, when it happened, and who did it. Frequently, parents are quite emotional by the time they get to the district level, and though that's easy to understand, they make a much better case by presenting facts.

Why do things get accomplished at the district level that don't at a lower level? It isn't that teachers or principals don't care; it's usually because a district administrator has an authority or an objective viewpoint that will allow him to accomplish what a teacher or principal could not. For example, recently a parent became frustrated because she felt that her child was not making sufficient progress in his special-education program. She contacted the teacher who said, "We conferenced about this two months ago at the start of school, and you agreed that this year your son would attend resource only twice a week, so that's all the time I saved for him. When we review the Individual Educational Plans in six months, then we can make changes if you're still unhappy." The parent felt this reasoning was absurd. Why should her child suffer for six months with too little instruction to help him. Furthermore, when she'd signed the IEP for reduced time, she'd done it at the special-education teacher's suggestion.

This parent's concern led her to the principal who said, "I'm sorry, but we do have to have procedures, and our special-education teacher is doing the best she can."

Still upset, the woman called the district office and spoke to the director of special education who agreed to research the situation and get back to her. "In this case," he said, "I felt the woman was right. Her son attends a fine school and the special-education teacher is excellent, but the child did need more time with her. She was feeling many other pressures, so I met with her to help her find a way to alter some things enough to be able to give this child additional help. Why could I do it when the principal couldn't? I guess in this case it is because special education is my whole background, and I could see some ways to reorganize some things that he might not have realized. Also, sometimes it helps to come in as an objective outsider."

THE PARENT

You may wonder what you're doing listed in a section on school resource people, but actually, you are a very important resource. You can serve as an initiator in helping your child get attention if there is a problem you feel needs to be checked. You can serve as a facilitator when communication has broken down or an appeal of a problem is needed, by going to the individual with the power to get it solved. Finally, you can serve as a system of checks and balances to make sure certain information is correct. Consider how this parent changed his child's schooling. A high school freshman honor student wanted to take chemistry without taking biology. Her counselor told her that she had to take biology because it was a state law. The child's father didn't think that sounded quite right, and so he called the state's Department of Education, which said no such law existed. Contacting the school, he explained what he had learned; he was issued an apology from the school, and his daughter signed up for the chemistry class she had wanted.

This story is not meant to denigrate the school system. Certainly I believe in the public schools, and I think the number of resources they offer is phenomenal. However, no one is infallible, and you can serve as one more check to make certain that your child gets the best.

*N*INE

YES, BUT WHAT ABOUT ALL THOSE OTHER QUESTIONS?

As Arizona's Teacher of the Year, I had the opportunity to speak with many people and to hear their concerns and questions about today's schools. Some issues surfaced repeatedly, and so this chapter is devoted to parents' questions about their children's school that haven't already been addressed elsewhere in the book.

BAD TEACHER

Q. My child has a bad teacher this year. She is unable to keep any real discipline in the classroom and so not much learning occurs. For various reasons, I can't get my child out of the class, and I can't get rid of the teacher. What do I do?

A. There is no denying that this is a bad situation. Here's how to make the best of it. First of all, if many parents in the class feel the way that you do, take things into your own hands, and improve the learning climate in the classroom. How? Develop a group of parents who are willing to work in the classroom as parent-aides. Tell your children that you are coming in to help the teacher, and you've all agreed to watch your own and the other children's behavior and tell their parents if it's bad. That way the teacher's weak disciplinary methods will be backed up by a strong parent. This will practically cut out all discipline problems.

Second, make sure that your children have responsibilities and expected rules of behavior at home. If they've been allowed to get away with making jokes at the expense of others, sassing authority, etc., the behavior will carry over to the school.

Third, keep working with other parents to focus the administration on the problems this teacher is having. The principal should be willing to work with the teacher to improve her discipline methods, which will not only benefit your child but other classes that follow.

If you cannot mobilize the concern or action of any other parents, that doesn't mean you need give up. Continue to pursue getting your child moved to another class. Don't make it a win-lose situation for anyone, just say that you think it would be a good idea for your child at this time. If at first you were turned down, try again. A blanket "no" is often the first response with the reason that children need to learn to get along in different situations with different personalities; however, in the long run, if you persist, most administrators will give in to the idea that your particular child needs a different situation in order to learn effectively.

Finally, consider this: The best or the worst teacher has your child for only about thirty hours a week. That still leaves around 130 hours outside of school each week. Even if eating, sleeping, and activities are included, he still spends a great deal of time with you, and your activities with him at home can be really significant in getting him through a bad year.

MAGNET SCHOOLS

Q. What is this magnet school I keep hearing about?

A. Magnet school is a term used throughout the country for an alternative school that offers some specific kind of education. It gets its name from the fact that children are drawn to it like a magnet. It can be an entire school or just a portion of a regular school. For example, in the Phoenix area there is a magnet school within a regular high school for students interested in fine arts. Expert teachers, additional resources, and advanced classes are available there that are not available in any other high school in the district.

Sometimes magnet schools are used as effective ways to implement integration. For example, by putting a highly desirable computer program at a magnet school that traditionally has faced "white flight," it is hoped that a number of students interested in this science will voluntarily return.

Sometimes magnet schools are created in order to maximize expertise in a particular academic area. There might not be enough students interested in advanced-physics programs to offer them at every school; however, if all the advanced-physics students attended one school, there might be enough to have a class.

There seems to be growing interest in the magnet concept. In Pittsburgh, parents stand in lengthy lines to vie for an enrollment spot for their child in some of the 19 district magnet programs. When the magnet concept was introduced to parents in 1979 only 1,500 students enrolled, but by 1986, 8,500 of the district's 40,000 pupils were involved in magnet programs.

CHEATING IN SCHOOL

Q. My child was caught cheating on a test. He claims that everyone is cheating in school today, and that I'm old-fashioned to get so upset. Just how common is student cheating?

A. There was a Junior Scholastic Survey of some 5,000 junior high students (NEA *Today's Education,* 1985, p. 70) that revealed some interesting information on this. It asked students if they'd ever cheated on a quiz or a test. The breakdown: 78 percent said never, 1 percent said often, the other 21 percent mentioned cheating sometimes or rarely. When asked why they did it, the biggest reason was that they were too lazy to study; next they said they did it to pass; and, finally, to get good grades.

As a teacher, let me say that in the world of education, cheating is just as unacceptable as it ever was. As a parent, I'd try to find out why my child cheated and deal with eliminating the reason. At any rate, I think you're right to be upset. When a child cheats, he's not only doing poorly on a test, but he is cheating himself. He is establishing por habits and a poor self-image.

MATH IN THE DARK AGES

Q. My son's math teacher won't let him use a calculator in the classroom. Why not, since the rest of the world uses them every day?

A. Granted, calculators are tremendous shortcuts and time-savers, but many math teachers would applaud your child's instructor's decision. They feel that calculators should not be used before it is absolutely certain that the student can solve problems on his own without the machine. Explains one high school advanced-math teacher, "I've gotten kids in my class who are supposed to have fine math minds, and yet, if the batteries in their calculators go dead, they're suddenly untrained in math. They can't subtract a simple problem without it. Parents who believe that it's unnecessary for their children to learn math facts *before* turning them loose on a calculator are turning them into functional math illiterates!"

DETENTION LIKE PRISON?

Q. Last week my son was truant from school. As punishment, the school assigned him after-school detention for a week. Won't this just make him hate school and want to be truant even more?

A. I don't know of any student who loves serving detention. However, I believe it serves a necessary purpose. There are many temptations for students to be truant. Let's face it, learning a new theorem may be more important, but it simply isn't as exciting to most kids as seeing the latest episode of their favorite soap opera. The same is true between a choice of learning how to write a coherent paragraph versus sitting in the sun to get a good tan before a big weekend dance. Kids don't often see the big picture, and so the school needs to make it very clear that truancy is unacceptable and there are definite consequences to being truant. In educational terms this is called negative reinforcement of behavior that one wishes to eradicate. In everyday language, it simply means that serving detention will probably make your child think twice before taking off from school again. As an added benefit, most schools insist that students spend their detention time quietly reading or doing homework, and for some who've had to do so, it's actually improved their studying and grades.

PEER TUTORING

Q. My child has been having some trouble in math, and the teacher has suggested letting another child be his tutor. What do you think about this idea?

A. Peer tutoring can be quite successful. In fact, according to a Stanford University study, it is more effective than computerized drill, reducing class size, or increasing instructional time (*Instructor* magazine, January 1985, p. 12).

There are several possible roadblocks to success. Try to find out how the child doing the tutoring was selected and how he feels about doing the tutoring. You will want to make certain that the child is both proficient in the skill himself and voluntarily offering his time. Also find out when the tutoring will be done and who will monitor it to check whether learning is actually taking place.

Once you've satisfied these requirements, I'd suggest you give peer tutoring a try. I've seen it work very successfully. There are numerous benefits. To begin with, it provides the child with a role model who likes the subject at a time when he is finding it difficult. This alone sometimes encourages a student not to give up because it can't be all that impossible. In addition, peer tutoring provides one-to-one instruction at no cost to the parent. Furthermore, no matter how much a teacher asks for questions, for some reason, kids are sometimes willing to ask other kids questions that they feel silly asking a teacher. Also, good friendships sometimes develop. If the method doesn't work, you can always try other alternatives, but I believe it is certainly worth a try.

NEW KINDS OF GROUP

Q. Our school has begun talking about "vertical grouping." What is this, and is it something we should try to prevent?

A. You probably didn't realize that up until now your child was involved in a "horizontal grouping" situation. This fancy term means that the child is in a classroom in which all the students are approximately the same age and all go through the same grade level at the same time. Vertical grouping means that children learn material as they are ready and chronological age is not important. Thus, if your third grader reads well, he might be in group with a couple of fourth graders and a fifth grader whose reading skills are a little low.

I don't know the actual situation at your school, but I don't believe vertical grouping is necessarily bad; ask to know why the school has decided to institute it, but I wouldn't immediately decide that I didn't want it just because it was something new.

WHY FAIL A CHILD?

Q. Our seventh-grade daughter's school just called to let us know that she would not pass, and she was going to be retained. I am very upset because she is physically very mature for her age, and I think she'll be embarrassed to be with younger children. How can I change the school's mind and get her promoted to be with her friends?

A. I would be very surprised if you can change the school's mind because with accountability becoming more and more of a factor, schools are frowning on the idea of social promotion. If your daughter hasn't mastered the material in seventh grade, do you really want her to go on to eighth grade?

As a parent, you might want to consider why she didn't pass seventh grade. Is she having academic problems which need attention? If so, I think I'd expend my energies trying to get her help instead of getting her passed. Promoting her only to be with her friends won't work; she'll feel more and more left out as they achieve and she can't.

Has she not passed because she didn't put forth much effort? Then as hard as it is for you as her parent, you must let her take the consequences of her actions. We've talked in an earlier chapter on discipline about kids who keep getting themselves into more and more serious trouble because they've come to believe that their parents will somehow be able to right whatever they've done wrong. If you attempt to have your daughter promoted when she's not done the work to deserve it, you're starting her on a road that you could regret. She will believe that she doesn't have to take responsibility for herself, and that school simply isn't very important because she was able to skip doing any work for a year and still succeed.

KIDS AND CRUELTY

Q. There is a boy in our neighborhood who is being tormented at school by the other kids. They're all calling him gay. It isn't true, but the boy is so upset that he wants to drop out of school. Why don't the teachers put a stop to this?

A. There are actually several questions here. Let's begin with the one about why teachers don't put a stop to the kids' cruelty. As a classroom teacher, I've found that I can certainly prevent any overt references within the confines of my classroom, and I can discuss the idea of what's wrong with using labels and/or rumors. I can have my students read stories about cruelty and have the kids discuss what its effects are and why being cruel is unfair and unjustified. Sometimes these things are enough to work. Unfortunately, they aren't infallible, and I've found that if a teacher goes beyond a certain point in trying to protect a child, the kids get to him in an even more vindictive way when her back is turned or when they are out of the classroom.

There are several things that I'd suggest you do to help this child. First of all, if this has gone on for only a few days, just have him ignore the taunts. Usually this is enough to have the perpetrators get tired of their game. It isn't easy for the victim, but it usually does work.

If this is an ongoing problem, try talking to the child's teachers to see if they are aware of it and to learn what they have done to try to stop it. Perhaps the teacher is not as aware of the situation as she might be and can take further action in her classroom to blunt the teasing. It might also be wise to have someone talk with the child about modifying certain behavior that could be fueling untrue rumors.

If you've already tried all these things, and nothing has worked, I would suggest considering letting the child transfer to another school. Kids can get stuck with labels that they cannot shake, and I've watched it actually interfere with their ability to do well in school. If there is no basis for the label, sometimes a new environment is all the child needs for a brand-new and much better beginning. However, before you make the switch, you have to make certain that the child isn't creating behavior which will immediately make the label reappear.

GOOD NEWS FOR PARENTS

Q. Why is it that the only time teachers contact parents is to let them know when their children have done something wrong? I don't have a genius child who makes straight A's, but he's a pretty good kid, and once in a while it would be nice to get a note home saying that he always does his homework or he showed good effort on a quiz.

A. You're right. It would be nice. Many schools are encouraging teachers to do this by giving them "Good-News Notes" or "Happy-Grams" to send to both parents and teachers. Teacher use of them increases when there is a semistandardized form to use. If your school doesn't have a Happy-Grams program, perhaps the PTA could make certain that each teacher has a ready supply of various kinds of good-news notes to use. Having a parents' club providing them would serve as a subtle reminder that parents would like to receive these messages, and with the notes at their fingertips, teachers would be more likely to get in the habit of using them.

THAT'S NOT HOW I DID MY HOMEWORK!

Q. My daughter has been coming to me with her math homework lately. I know how to get the answers, but not the way her book explains it. My method has worked fine for me. Is it all right if I just teach her the way I learned?

A. Begin to help your daughter by letting her work through the problem as you try to follow the logic of the way the process is being presented. If it doesn't make sense to you, suggest she get help from another student or see her teacher.

It's understandably frustrating to want to help, know you can get to the solution, and not give it to your child. However, the new path to the solution might actually create more of a problem to a confused student. She will receive no reinforcement at school of the way you're teaching, and no reinforcement when she's home of the method she's supposed to be learning at school. Frequently, students begin to intermix the two and come out with a third method that doesn't work at all. The situation reminds me of a woman who wanted to make a perfect sponge cake. She called two different friends to ask each her recipe, then decided to combine elements of both. The resulting cake was a complete flop.

IT'S SUMMERTIME AND THE READING IS GREAT

Q. How can I get my kids to read during the summer? They don't pick up a book between May and September.

A. First of all, it's excellent that you recognize the importance of their reading during the summer. The results are well worth the effort. Barbara Heys, in her book *Summer Learning and the Effects of School* (Academic Press), reports that:

- The number of books read during the summer is consistently related to achievement gains.

- Reading is the single summer activity most strongly and consistently related to summer learning.

- Children in every income group who read six or more books over the summer gained more in reading achievement than children who did not.

Of course, that only shows that summer reading has an important place in the learning process. How can you get your child involved? Try these suggestions.

Give him a couple of books you think he'll like as an end-of-the-school-year present.

Investigate the library programs in your community. Many of them offer summer book clubs for children with awards and rewards for books read. They also offer a number of interesting summer programs including magic shows, movies, craft classes, etc. that will hopefully stimulate your child's interest in the activity enough to want to check out one of the books suggested at the program's end. For example, your reluctant reader may be fascinated enough with a magic show to want to read a book telling him how the tricks were done.

If the child is past a very primary reading level, you might try this approach: Have the whole family go to the library and pick out a book that they think everyone in the family would enjoy. After everyone finishes his book, he exchanges it with another member of the family. To many children, reading becomes far more interesting if they have someone with whom they can discuss the book's characters and situations. Also, there is something very appealing to most kids in picking out a book their parents have to read.

Don't be embarrassed to have family read-alouds. Your children are never too old for this activity, and an interesting book read with some feeling and drama is the best advertisement in the world for how much fun reading can be.

Designate a half hour a day as family reading time in which everyone must read something. The TV can't be on, phone calls will have to be returned later, etc. Don't be too restrictive about what your child is reading during that time as long as he's reading. Sure, you'd rather it be quality literature than comic books, but comic books will improve reading skills better than nothing at all.

DOES MY CHILD NEED A COMPUTER TO PASS?

Q. My son came home the other day and said that his English teacher said that kids who had computers were much better writers. I don't know much about how computers operate, and I wonder if this is true.

A. Until computers can think for human beings, computers cannot produce writing. That must come from within your son's brain. The computer is a tool just like a typewriter which may make his writing easier to read, but it cannot do the writing for him.

Your son may have only understood part of what the teacher was saying. I know that personally I'd like to see every one of my English students have access to a computer/word processor. It doesn't make them better writers, but it does make them much more willing to experiment, revise, and rewrite. Let me give you an example. I had two students working on short stories they ultimately wanted to enter in writing contests. The first child had a word processor. I suggested modifying little parts of characterization in several places and changing a couple of key parts of dialogue. "Great," said the student, "I think that would be better. I'll type in the changes and press a button that prints out the corrected story. How about if I bring it in tomorrow? Then if you think it needs more changes, I'll try if differently."

The second student had neatly written everything in pen. When I suggested changes to him, he shook his head. "I don't really think it's that bad. If I change those things, then I'm going to have to rewrite the whole paper, and it took me forever to get this one neat enough."

The story speaks for itself. Does a computer make a child a writer? Absolutely not. Does it make him more willing to experiment and make changes in editing? In my experience, definitely so.

A VACATION DURING SCHOOL

Q. February is the only time my husband can get away this year, so we're going to take a family vacation during school. Will my son be penalized for this?

A. Rule for compulsory attendance vary from school district to school district. In many there are now rules stating that students will be dropped from the school after missing a designated number of school days a semester, so the place to begin is by finding out what the exact rules are for your district.

After you've done that and decided that you can still take the vacation there are several things to do. First talk with your son. Explain that your taking this vacation at this time is a result of circumstances but that you feel his schooling is very important. Let him know that you will work with him, but that it will be necessary for him to make every effort to complete all the work he misses. Unless you clearly indicate otherwise, your child may interpret taking a family vacation during school as meaning that school just isn't that important. You can imagine why the teacher had an attitude problem with the girl who told her, "Yeah, we're going to Florida for a couple of weeks. My mom doesn't like to go during spring break because it's too crowded, and my dad doesn't like to go in the summer because it's too humid." Whether or not it was true, this girl perceived climate as more important in her parents' eyes than her education.

Be certain you or your child (depending on his age) contacts his teachers and asks them ahead of time for any work that he can do while he is gone. Then be sure that he takes the proper books and supplies on the trip to complete the assignments. Nothing irritates a teacher more than to prepare a week's worth of assignments and instructions only to find out that the student has never touched any of the material.

If you know that you will be gone, have your child do any long-term assignments well in advance of your leaving. That way he can concentrate on making up what he's missing.

Finally, even the best student finds it hard to be dedicated to school on vacation. Help your child by building study time into the trip; don't depend on him to figure out when to squeeze it in, and try not to wait until he's so tired that he can't make sense of what he is doing. One of my best students this year took a week to go camping and hunting with his father. His parents were divorced and that was the only time his dad could take him. When he returned, the boy told me that he'd never forget the trip or the memories of his dad. "But, Mrs. Fields," he added, "you'll be happy to know that every night just before we started getting the fire going for dinner, my dad made me study for a while." He handed me all of his assignments and said proudly, "I got everything done."

Although sometimes scheduling trips to coincide with school vacations can't be done and although it is certainly true that children can learn vast amounts on vacation, please don't make a habit of being gone frequently during school. The child does lose continuity with what's going on in the classroom. Besides, there is a high correlation between good attendance and high achievement.

TEACHER REQUESTS

Q. I don't have any say as to which teacher my child will have next year because of a "no-request" policy at his school. Why would a school do such a thing, and is there a way to get around it?

A. Many schools have adopted a no-request policy in recent years. It's easy to see why this would be confusing to parents who hear that their participation in their child's school is encouraged and then rejected when it comes time for teacher selection. So why are schools adhering to such a policy? One principal explains, "There is a great deal of thought that goes into providing the best educational climate for your child. For example, we try to balance classes in terms of equalizing the number of boys and girls, we try to minimize the possibility for discipline problems by separating children who seem to egg each other on to negative behavior. We see how the child acts and interacts and try to match him with the teacher who can best motivate him to successful learning."

Teacher requests can create a real morale problem among the staff when a particular teacher gets a reputation as being good and the majority of requests are for her. Sometimes, those requests come in without a great deal of thought or research. One very popularly requested teacher developed a reputation among the kids as being the "best one in the whole third grade." Why? She gave the children an extra ten minutes of free time/recess when the rest of the classes were doing science.

Every parent wants his child to have a "good" teacher, but what connotes good? For the neighbor whose child is somewhat unruly it might be a very strict, no-nonsense disciplinarian. For your child it might be a warm, supportive, easygoing person. A school geared for success will take these things into mind when placing your child with his teacher for the following year.

In other words, much of the time it seems parent requests are not based on enough research to matter. However, I still believe that if you are an involved parent who knows what is happening at your child's school and who has a definite feeling about whom your child should have for his teacher the following year, it's worth it to circumvent the no-request policy. The first way is to talk to your child's current teacher. Frequently, she is the one who will make the decision as to where to place your child for the following year. A chat with her about your desires and reasons for them will usually result in her placing the child where you want him.

If the current teacher has no say-so, then it is worth it to make an appointment with the principal. Explain that though you are aware of the no-request policy, you know that his and your goal are the same—to give your child the best education possible. Don't denigrate the other teachers, just explain why you feel that a particular teacher would best meet your child's needs. Chances are excellent that your request will be granted, regardless of the official policy, because most other parents won't have pursued the matter in such a logical, well-informed, persistent way.

A MOVING QUESTION

Q. We are going to move to a new city soon. Though I've researched the new school, and it seems excellent, my children are most upset. Do kids who change schools in the middle of the year adjust all right, and is there anything I can do to help them?

A. Yes to both questions! Many students who've come into my class from other schools find that by the end of the year, they can't imagine why they were ever so upset about having to move, so don't be discouraged. There are several things you can do to help ensure the success of the move. First of all, your attitude can make a tremendous difference. Are you approaching the move as an exciting adventure or a chin-up kind of punishment that must be done? Children often adopt their parents' attitudes, so be positive about the new situation. It's perfectly fine, however, to sympathize with your children about leaving their old friends.

As a parent, you will probably find that you need to be more concerned about a primary-grade child's academic adjustment, and a secondary child's social adjustment. A child in the early grades is learning basic skills that he will need to make him successful throughout the rest of his school experiences. Before you leave your child's former school, write down what texts he was using, collect several samples of his reading and math papers, and ask his teacher if she'd write a summary of approximately where they are in math, reading, writing, and other subjects at the time your child is leaving. Take this material with you when you enroll your child in his new school, and find out if the classes he's entering will be using approximately the same material. One bright sixteen-year-old I have confessed to me that she was rotten at subtraction. "We moved when I was in the second grade; my old class was just starting subtraction when I left; my new class had just finished it and was starting multiplication, so I never really learned subtraction in school."

Watch your child's work as he begins to bring it home from his new school. If you suspect that it is much different from what he had been doing at his previous school, make an appointment with his new teacher. Ask her if there are some things you can do at home to help him better fit into the academic program at this school.

With secondary students, you still want to keep an eye on academic placement and make certain you bring complete records when the child enrolls in his new school. However, teens have had more years in school than primary youngsters to adjust to different teachers and teaching styles. Additionally, they are only with any one teacher for less than an hour a day. Unfortunately, teens have terribly fragile egos and fear of being unaccepted socially can prevent academic achievement. If possible, give your child a sense of self-confidence by letting him see the school before he actually enrolls. Little things like his knowing what kind of clothes and school supplies the kids have will ease his transition into the school.

Don't expect instant adjustment. It is hard to be new at a time when he's already feeling uncertain of himself. Don't be alarmed if your usually gregarious child has turned suddenly shy. As one boy told me, "When I first moved here, I decided I'd rather be a nothing than a nerd, so I didn't say anything for a while."

Encourage your teen to get involved in the new community whether it be in a church group, school club, or both. These extra-curricular activities provide a way for your child to instantly be part of a social group without having to risk doing the actual inviting. One girl last year entered our school and joined the Spanish Club just as it was making its homecoming banner. She immediately found herself at someone's house stuffing crepe paper into chicken wire with about twenty other kids. After five or six days of this, she felt she knew some of the kids well enough to invite them over, and others she at least felt she knew enough to say hi to in the hallways at school. Suddenly, she wasn't so alone any more.

KINDERGARTEN EINSTEIN?

Q. I heard that in my school district, my child has to pass a test to get into kindergarten. Why?

A. Kindergarten today is much more academic than when you and I were there. In fact, kindergarteners do much of the work that was not given to us until we were in the first grade. To make certain that a child is developmentally ready to handle this, some school districts give tests. There is nothing wrong with your child if he does not pass the test. Children sometimes just need the extra year before they are ready to do the work. If they are pushed ahead, they often develop academic and behavior problems throughout school.

Once the child is in school, no one pays any attention to whether he started at five or six. There's a much greater chance for his accomplishment in school if he enters school a year later than if he has to be retained later on in his schooling. Whether or not your child is delayed a year shouldn't be a light decision. Talk with the people who tested your child for kindergarten. If he's been in pre-school, talk to his preschool teacher as well. Ask for explanations, and don't be afraid to ask questions, but do be realistic. One father who'd had everything carefully explained to him, looked at the school principal, shook his finger, and announced, "Every Johnson kid enters school at five, and this one will too."

Check to see if your school offers a prekindergarten class or a prefirst-grade class. More and more schools are showing an interest in both as a means of providing the right environment for a child who is not quite ready to go on yet.

MY GIFTED CHILD

Q. Not too long ago, I was notified that my child had been designated as highly gifted. I've heard of enrichment and acceleration programs—what would be best for my child?

A. You need to make an appointment to speak with the resource teacher who deals with the gifted at your child's school. She can give you a detailed explanation of what she can offer your child. However, here is some important general information.

Gifted kids are like any other children in that they need lots of love and affection. Parents sometimes make the mistake of thinking that just because their child is quite bright, he is also quite mature, which is not necessarily true. Don't expect perfection.

Intellectually gifted children need encouragement to explore areas in which they aren't gifted. They get used to "winning," and become afraid to try anything in which they might lose. They can deal with abstract ideas at an earlier age than other children, and they thrive on parental stimulation that encourages learning. They don't necessarily hate school, but they can become bored and unmotivated if they are not challenged. There are two philosophies about how to keep them challenged. One is that gifted children should be allowed to be in an *acceleration* program in which they learn material as they are ready for it, and no attempt is made to keep them on the same grade level as their peers. In other words, why keep them in the third-grade reader if they already know the skills being taught in it, just because the rest of the class is still there? Let the gifted child keep advancing to more difficult material.

Those who support *enrichment* say that it is important to keep gifted kids on the same social level as their peers and that even though they have the academic ability, they lack the maturity to handle some of the higher skills until they are older. Thus, why not allow the gifted child to use his reading ability to finish his third-grade reading assignment quickly and then work on turning the story into a play?

Having a child who is gifted is a joy in many ways, but it is a big responsibility. The lingering attitude that "they'll learn anyway," sometimes leaves classes of the gifted short of materials and resources. There is often a stigma among the kids about being "too smart," and it is true that the second highest drop-out rate is among the talented and gifted. You can help your child achieve his full potential by staying involved in his school, supplementing his curiosity at home, and joining your state association for the gifted and talented. An excellent book for parents of gifted children: *The Gifted*

Child, the Family, and the Community, Bernard S. Miller and Merle Price, eds. (New York: Walker and Co., 1981).

PROBLEM WITH TEACHERS TODAY

Q. I went to a rural school when I was growing up. The teacher had several grades in the same room; she had to take care of the school building, and she never complained. Today's teachers don't seem to have to do half the work, but they never seem happy. What's wrong with them?

A. There are several elements commonly thought to affect job satisfaction. One is the prestige with which the job is regarded in the community. Yet many teachers feel their occupation is given little respect by the public. An indication of this is found in a Gallup Poll that asked respondents whether they'd want to have a child of theirs teach in the public schools as a career. In 1969, 75 percent of the respondents said yes, but by 1983 that figure had dropped to 45 percent. Parents want the best teachers for their children, but they don't want their children to become teachers. That message comes through loud and clear. Kids bring with them to the classroom an attitude that teaching is a profession for those who can't or won't do something that makes more money.

That brings up the whole question of money which, of course, is another element of job satisfaction. Two 1984 studies show a great disparity between the average starting salary for teachers and those of comparable professions requiring the same level of education. Teaching was 33 percent below even the lowest other field researched, and more than $10,000 a year lower than a profession like engineering.* One teacher put it in more specific terms. He said, "I watch my students come to class in designer jeans and talk about going away to camp for the whole summer. My kids wear hand-me-downs and we camp out as a family because that's all we can afford."

---

* NEA, *Today's Education,* 1985, p. 68.

At least 125,000 teachers are threatened with physical violence each month. Seventy-five percent of urban teachers and 40 percent of rural teachers are cursed at by students every month. Most frightening are the statistics that show that a quarter of all teachers nationwide have been assaulted at least once, and for 40 percent of all teachers violence is a daily concern and a constant fear.*

Finally, there is what seems to be an ever increasing workload. Teacher stress is so high that some schools are suggesting special seminars for teachers on how to cope. I've seen a tremendous explosion in the paperwork required of teachers in terms of record-keeping and attendance. The average high school teacher deals with 150 to 170 students per day. That means that if he gives an assignment just every other day that needs to be graded and that assignment is only two pages in length, in a five-day week, he will take home at least 900 pages of work to be graded.

In 1779, the Encyclopedia Britannica was three volumes, and that was all the information known to man. Now it's possible to keep the encyclopedia on computer to constantly update the many changes in the vast storehouse of information. Our knowledge base and the amount of information that we need to teach is increasing at an extremely great rate, yet at the same time, the schools are also trying to tackle many problems that parents once took care of themselves. Health information, driver's education, vision and hearing screening, vocational and college information, special ability screening, etc. take up time as well. With more two-parent working families and latchkey kids, children stay around school just to talk. Explains one first-grade teacher, "I used to be able to get a lot of my lesson planning done after school, but Manuel's mother works until nine at night. His parents are divorced, and he stays after school to keep me company. I feel so guilty if I brush him aside and go ahead with my work that I stay at school with him as long as I can and take the extra workload home."

---

* David Brooks, "Order in the Classroom," *National Review,* December 13, 1985, p. 24.

I invite anyone who thinks being a fine teacher is an easy job today to try it for even a week. That's not to say we, in the field, don't love what we are doing. In spite of its drawbacks, being a teacher is a tremendously exciting job. It's a profession that believes in the future; that says we want to help children explore the world of learning and give them the opportunity to achieve their dreams. We need to know when we are doing something wrong; we need to be told when our work needs improvement, but we also need to hear from parents when they feel that we've had a positive impact on their children's lives.

*T*EN

HATS OFF TO SOME SUPER SCHOOLS

In any given month there is enough negative material published about America's public schools to make the average parent despair. There is no doubt that our educational system is not perfect, and the media has made certain that everyone has heard what's wrong. That's fine; certainly we need to correct the flaws in education, but unfortunately, what's right about our schools often goes unstated, which makes it quite hard for parents to get a balanced picture. I believe it's only fair to present the other side of the coin. Let me reassure you that there are a great many wonderful aspects of education happening every day in public schools around the country. To call attention to at least some of the unheralded excellence that is taking place in today's schools, the U.S. Department of Education has begun an official school-recognition program, and the qualifications for selection are not easy. Schools must first be nominated by their state education agency and then pass a difficult screening and site visit. Secondary schools have been recognized for the past several years, and elementary schools joined them in 1986.

WHAT MAKES A SCHOOL MARVELOUS?

Much research and study has been done to find the common traits in America's most successful schools, and one heartening fact that has come from all this is that you really don't have to pick up stakes and move to find a good school. Your child's school doesn't have to be a particular size or be located in any particular area of the country for it to qualify as one of the best. However, there are some characteristics that have been discovered in winning schools. As an involved parent, you may wish to find out if similar types of attitudes and programs exist in your school. If not, you may want to work on ways to institute them. As a concerned citizen, you can certainly be reassured by the innovation and excellence that some schools have already achieved. The U.S. Department of Education program has recognized high schools for three years and much data has been gathered about common traits they share. (Because elementary schools have just begun to be cited by the program, similar data is not yet available for them.) According to *The Search for Successful Secondary Schools: The First Three Years of the Secondary Schools Recognition Program,** exceptional schools are particularly strong in the areas of extracurricular participation, recognition of student behavior and performance, school climate, rates of student and teacher attendance, attention to academic learning time, teacher efficacy, and community support.

Schools that have been found to be extraordinarily successful are more tightly managed than most. Everyone in such schools agrees on the goals and the work given is well directed toward achieving those goals. Because they are such strong schools with clear purpose, they make greater academic demands on their students. This has reduced the negative effects of a poor socioeconomic background and/or negative peer pressure on student achievement.

America's finest schools' written goals don't differ greatly from those of most schools; however, in the winning schools, goals are taken seriously and translated into daily action. For example, the report cites a school that states, "The vision of this school is to use the scientific process as a fundamental learning strategy, a means through which to develop critical thinking and problem-solving

---

*(Research for Better Schools, Washington, D.C.: GPO, October 1986.)

skills, and a method for use in gathering and organizing data." That sounds like a hefty agenda, and to keep it from being just words, the school board worked with the local Zoological Society to build a school on the zoo grounds. Students have had the opportunity to observe a bison give birth and to watch an animal autopsy. They are not just studying science in the classroom but applying it to a living laboratory.

Successful schools are led by good principals. Principals of successful schools understand their communities, make people feel welcome at the school, and know how to work with community members. The principal is trusted and respected because it is honestly believed by students, parents, and teachers that even if they don't agree with his decisions, his only purpose in making them is to serve the interests of the school.

If you are wondering how effective the principal is at your child's school, you might like to know that the single quality most often cited by parents, teachers, and students in award-winning schools for their principal is fairness, and the ability to base his decisions on what is best for student welfare. In addition, the report found that good principals have the ability to recognize the strengths of all the people on their staffs and help those people maximize the use of their particular skills.

In the nomination form for the School Recognition Program, students in both junior and senior high schools overwhelmingly say that the quality of the teachers is the most important thing in making their schools good schools. In very successful schools, it has been found that there's a low turnover of teachers. Those who are teaching at the school feel a tremendous sense of pride in *their* school. One nomination form says that their school staff meets, discusses exactly what should be required of them, and reinforces each other in having high expectations and demanding excellent performance. Teachers who don't want to put in that time and dedication feel as if they don't fit in with the other teachers at this school.

From the research done, it appears that you can increase your chances of staffing your child's school with fine teachers if you have a good principal there; if the teachers feel physically safe teaching in the school; if the physical plant is in fairly good condition; and if the feeling of the community and administration is one that says that teachers count. As one nomination form explains, "Our teachers feel that they play the critical role in curriculum development and review."

Once a staff begins to be filled with good teachers, it attracts more of the same. Word gets around that this is a stimulating environment in which professional excellence is rewarded. In fact, here are some of the ways that various top schools recognize their teachers.

- Graduating seniors honor a teacher by asking her to read their names at the graduation ceremony.

- A PTA sponsors a project in which parents are encouraged to compliment teachers on things they do well.

- Outstanding teachers are invited as speakers at a special lecture series open to parents and the community. Students then see their parents voluntarily going to attend speeches by their teachers.

- Each faculty meeting begins by discussing all the positive things that occurred during the previous week. Staff members freely praise each other at these meetings.

Sometimes schools choose to honor outstanding teachers monetarily. Outstanding Teacher Awards are given to ten teachers yearly in one school. Selected by a vote of peers, students, and administrators, each teacher is awarded $100. Another school has had a merit-pay plan for twenty-five years. Teachers enter the plan voluntarily and can earn up to $2000 in merit pay.

In many of the nomination forms there is discussion of recognition of teachers by notes from parents and former students.

It's felt that students work harder if they have good relationships with the adults in the school. However, with 150 to 175 students per day, teachers often find it difficult to make close connections. Some of the more successful schools recognize this factor and build in interaction outside the classroom. For example, in one school each teacher is also an advisor who watches over five to ten students in a highly structured program of communication and monitoring of academics, attendance, and behavior. Kids may feel that teachers have high standards, but they also feel that the teachers are supportive and caring and very much want for them to succeed.

The Secondary School Recognition Report shows evidence that there is a definite link between student involvement and student success in school, and that's why it is, perhaps, no surprise that one winning high school offers at least forty active extracurricular organizations in addition to a complete girls' and boys' athletic program. At least 85 percent of the student body participates in one or more of these activities. There is a feeling of pride in not wanting to rush off the minute the last bell rings—there's still too much to do at school.

In another winning school the emphasis on extracurricular activities is so great that the school says, "You tell us about an area of interest, and if we don't already have a club, we will help find you an advisor and you can start a club."

The Search for Successful Secondary Schools: The First Three Years of the Secondary School Recognition Program (p. 83) explains, "Participation builds a sense of belonging and a sense of accomplishment that are essential to maturation. .. .. fit is not a new approach nor a novel one, but it is tried, tested, and it works."

Schools cited as outstanding have high expectations for their students. One said, "Students are no longer allowed to select academic classes which are below their ability level. Four years ago, students completed their own schedules and were allowed to select courses satisfying the minimum requirements. Now students and parents receive individualized counseling prior to scheduling."

It is important to realize that as school becomes more demanding, it is necessary to provide stronger rewards and recognition of achievement. Many of the very successful schools have ceremonies and "Halls of Fame" for students who do well academically. Each month in one high school, a different academic department has the chance to select twenty-four students worthy of recognition. These students are invited to a luncheon, served a fine meal, and after the meal they are praised for their accomplishments.

In another school, students who raise their grade point by .5 from the previous semester or who maintain a 3.85 grade-point average can get a special card good for two paid admissions to athletic games and one admission to a fine-arts activity. The specific program doesn't seem nearly as important as the fact that some kind of very special activities exist that promote student motivation toward achievement.

Successful schools have a high percentage of parental involvement both in the classroom and in the rest of the community. For example, one high school has parents who've produced a videotape describing the school and its programs. Believing that education is everyone's business, and that people are much more likely to relinquish tax dollars for education if they know what's being done in schools, these parents volunteer to show the videotape to any group in the community who is interested in seeing it. Since much of the community doesn't have children in school, the parents take the school to them to find allies in education.

This is not to say that even the most successful of schools don't have their share of problems—they do, but they look at their problems not as insurmountable barriers, but as a rock in the road that there must somehow be a way around. Overall, however, it seems the most pervasive problem is lack of funds. Even in the most outstanding of schools there are almost constant reports of good programs, fine extracurricular activities, and excellent resource programs having to be cut. One principal expressed the opinion that there will be no answer to this problem until his city honors its commitment to its high schools and does something to reduce class size and protect programs by approving more taxes to be spent for schools.

There would be no way to summarize all of the outstanding programs that are occurring in schools across the country, but here are a few that I felt were not only very worthwhile, but also might be things you could implement in your school. Some of these schools have received awards for their programs; others have not yet been recognized.

CHEERS FOR ACADEMIC SUCCESS

Among kids, it has always been acceptable and even desired to be the fastest runner or the best basketball player. Yet the student who consistently scores the highest on tests or raises his hand the most with the answers is often given no positive feedback from his peers. That's not true at Ann Arbor Huron High School in Ann Arbor, Michigan. Each year, they hold an academic pep rally on the Friday before the Advanced Placement exams to recognize the school's scholars and boost their spirits in preparation for upcoming exams. It's a concept that could be translated to any school. Why should we cheer only the athletes?

TIME FOR MORE LEARNING IN THE SCHOOL DAY

Benjamin Cardozo High School in Bayside, New York, decided that students needed to spend more time on task. But the school day was a fixed length, so how could they suddenly find more time? This school found several solutions which might work in your child's school too. They decreased the length of class-passing time and added the minutes to the length of the period. They decreased the length of homeroom period. Testing and survey days that previously took an entire day were reduced to half days and classes were held for the remainder of the time. When it could be done, teachers were encouraged to place homework assignments on prepared handout sheets rather than taking the time to write them on the chalkboard. The policy allowing school social trips to be taken on school days was changed so that the trips could be taken only during vacation time. How much difference could all these things make?

Even if all these policies increased the length of time spent on actual teaching by only five minutes a day (and it's likely that the time was more), the total adds up to over an additional 1,000 minutes of instruction per year at no additional cost to taxpayers.

A PLACE OF PRIDE

At Walter White Elementary School in Ceres, California, visitors feel the sense of pride these children have in their school. Because kids care about their school, they want to be there and they want to succeed there. What is Walter White doing to make them feel this way? Actually, the ideas are quite simple. For one thing, the school assigns each class an area on the grounds to keep clean. If the area isn't clean, the yard-inspection team gives them penalties. If the areas are clean for two months, they get a ribbon. Most of the classes sport ribbons proudly.

Kids have a chance to feel part of the decision-making process as well. The fifth graders spent two weeks taking a lunch survey of all the students and teachers. They came up with favorite menus, and then they worked with the cafeteria staff to determine nutritional needs. The kids learned a lot, got to put their academics to practical use, and came up with a week of menus that were actually used by the cafeteria.

WHERE READING AND WRITING
SPELL EXCITEMENT

If you're wondering how to inject some creativity and excitement into your school's reading and writing programs, you might consider patterning the school after Scenic Hills Elementary School in Springfield, Pennsylvania. The school has a Mystery Reader program that uses the community to demonstrate to students that reading is a priority in life, and "everyone" reads. Mystery Readers are interested citizens, parents, and special area teachers who are invited guest readers in individual classrooms. The mystery is that students don't know who the readers are or when they are coming. (Teachers do, however, so that the time is budgeted into lesson plans.) There is an air of excitement as a Mystery Reader enters the classroom, and all other activity stops immediately. With the assistance of the librarian, this program has become an excellent way to introduce the newest good reading in the library to students.

The school also has a newspaper club open to third and fourth graders. They are responsible for putting out a school newspaper. "Reporters" find their own stories and write them with help only on spelling, punctuation, and capitalization. The students type their stories into computers, and print them out on printers. They illustrate the paper with pencil drawings. The kids are responsible for the paper's layout and design, and when finished, they photocopy the paper. The reporters then complete their final task, delivery to each classroom.

If that sounds complex for eight- and nine-year-olds to attempt, then perhaps you should know about their television show. Called *Kids' News,* new programs are taped twice weekly, and each class is responsible for the stories on a show, including writing and video clips. Each child is responsible for a job, and each child has a chance to do the jobs of camera, switcher, sound, reporter, and assistant. The show is seen throughout the school and the community via cablevision daily. Two new shows and three reruns weekly give everyone a chance to see the final product.

ATHLETICS AND ACADEMICS *DO* MIX AT THIS SCHOOL

In many high schools throughout the country, there has been a great deal of controversy over whether some student athletes are learning anything besides sports, but in West Ottawa High School in Holland, Michigan, they've devised an extracurricular eligibility policy that's working well. All student athletes, band members, debate-club participants, student-council officers, etc., are required to pass a minimum of four classes with at least a C −. If a student falls short of this minimum, he is put on three weeks probation and assigned a tutor who can be either a teacher or an honor student. The student on probation remains a member of the team or club for the next three weeks, allowed to fully participate in every activity. However, if after that time of tutoring he has not raised his grades, he loses his team membership but continues working with the tutor. His membership is reinstated when the grade meets the requirements.

Principal Tom Updegraff says, "The policy is designed to improve learning rather than to penalize kids, and it is working. At the present time, not one student has had to be dropped from an organization or a sport."

A CLASS TO SERVE THE COMMUNITY

At Santa Fe Technical High School in Santa Fe, New Mexico, both community and student needs are well served by a preschool-education class that is taught by Aileen Garcia and exists to give high school students the opportunity to develop responsible skills for working with young children, to prepare for parenting and/or careers involving the care and welfare of young children. The theories learned in the classroom about child development are not just tucked away somewhere, for the students actually operate a four-day-a-week preschool on the high school campus. Each high schooler in the program is head teacher twice a month which means he is responsible for making detailed lesson plans for those days. The rest of the month he is an assistant teacher in music, art, science, etc. Each Monday, the "teachers" meet to work on projects and do observation reports. The high schoolers are seeing the immediate impact of what they've learned, and the preschool shares something in common with America's most prestigious private preschools: Parents feel the education good enough to put their names on an extensive waiting list.

AN OPEN DOOR FOR MATH HELP

Remember trying to work a math problem and feeling so frustrated that you never wanted to see another number? At Lowell High School in San Francisco, California, kids haven't had to face that kind of frustration. Taking advantage of a modular-programming schedule that allows students pockets of free time throughout the school day, the teachers in the Lowell Math Department established an open-door tutoring program. A room designated just for tutoring is continually staffed throughout the day by members of the math department so that any student wishing help from algebra to calculus can drop by during his free time. Not only does it provide for one-on-one professional tutoring the instant a student gets confused, but it allows him to hear the explanation in a slightly different way than his own teacher would have given it, which may make the concept clearer.

If you as a parent would like to see a similar setup in your school, talk with its administrators. It's possible that parents with good math backgrounds could even help staff the center.

A WELCOMING ATMOSPHERE

Imagine what it feels like to be the new kid in school after the year has started. You're the only one who can't find his locker; you're the only one who doesn't know how to get to your next class, or have anyone with whom to eat lunch. It's a great way to get a student started off on the wrong foot. That's why Sunnyslope High School in Phoenix, Arizona, has established a special group of student ambassadors. This select group is chosen based on citizenship, academics, and involvement in school. One of these school ambassadors greets each new student, meets him after every one of his classes on his first day at school, and shows him the way to his next class. In addition, these Sunnyslope High School student ambassadors share information about extracurricular activities and explain how to become a participant in them. New students leave their first day feeling positive about themselves and about the opportunities at their new school.

POSITIVE ACTION TO KEEP KIDS
OUT OF TROUBLE

In schools across the country there has been much concern over the numbers of teens who've gotten pregnant, attempted suicide, or been involved in substance abuse. At Hazen High School in Hazen, North Dakota, that concern has translated itself into positive action that's helping kids stay out of trouble. The school implemented a Peer Support Group in April of 1982 which has proven to be quite beneficial.

Teens are chosen for the Peer Support Group on the basis of their leadership qualities, positive peer relations, and receptiveness to learning. The group has thirty members each year, and students are selected throughout grades 7 through 12. Qualified experts speak to this group and the group then reaches out to the rest of the student body to disseminate important information that might not be listened to if it came from an adult. The group has also proven itself able to respond to the needs of other students experiencing difficulty with a problem in their lives. Friends helping other friends is the philosophy of the program.

AN IRRESISTIBLE CHALLENGE TO READ

In Lake Havasu City, Arizona, 272 elementary school children at Nautilus Elementary read over 11,000 books last year. What a sight it was to see kids lined up at the school waiting for the doors to open so that they could be the first ones at the library to check out more books.

What created this sudden love of reading? It was a creative principal who strolled into a busy lunchroom one day, sat down at a middle table, and began to read. A hush fell among the students as word spread that the principal was there. "What are you doing, Mr. Conley?" ventured one brave student.

"I'm reading," he said. "Shh, this is a good book, and I don't want to be disturbed." The next day he reappeared in the same spot sporting a big button that said, "You Can't Do It!" Answering no questions, he continued to read his book. Curiosity spread like wildfire and soon every child wanted to know what he couldn't do. Finally, the principal told them: He didn't think they could read 11,000 books by the end of the year. By that time they were ready to prove they could do whatever he thought they couldn't. Soon the walls of the entire school were covered with names and numbers of books read, and by the end of the school year, the kids gleefully announced that the principal was wrong and they were right. They told him he'd lost and they'd won, but in reality, everyone had won —his pupils had read 11,180 books.

Of course, this is but a small sampling of the good things that are going on in today's schools. What they prove is that creativity and excellence in public education are available. As a concerned parent, you should not hesitate to explore ideas you think could make your child's school a better one or to let people know about the good things that are going on at your child's school.

APPENDIX

The following are resource organizations that may be helpful to parents.

National Committee for Citizens in Education
10840 Little Patuxent Parkway
Suite 301
Columbia, Maryland 21044-2396
1-800-NET-WORK

NCCE was founded in 1973 and dedicated to improving public schools through public involvement. NCCE provides a toll-free hot-line for parents to call about school-related problems and offers a number of pamphlets for purchase concerning school issues.

National School Volunteer Program, Inc. (NSVP)
701 N. Fairfax Street
Suite 320
Alexandria, Virginia 22314
(703) 836-4880

NSVP publishes a newsletter, develops and publishes training manuals for volunteers, and presents programs to help school systems set up volunteer programs or create and manage business/education partnerships. Individuals interested in volunteering in schools are encouraged to join.

The group quotes Ronald Reagan as saying, "The National School Volunteer Program is composed of dedicated citizens who are ready to lend a helping hand to develop our most precious resource—America's children."

The National PTA
700 N. Rush St.
Chicago, IL 60611-2571
(312) 787-0977

There are more than 5.6 million PTA members today in 24,000 local schools. The purpose of PTA is for "parents and teachers together to carry out programs to improve the lives, health and safety of our nation's children, and to help them become productive citizens in our democratic society."

The national organization offers a number of booklets and pamphlets for purchase.

INDEX